Rock Your Light is a soul activatic
It's a guide of potent and powerful le:
their big heart work in this world. Thr
compelling and fresh insights blended wit
cultivate the trust, courage and purpose t
you've been gifted. Infused with Tracey'
huge heart, *Rock Your Light* is a book that will ignite the inner
knowing that you're on the perfect path. This is THE book
you'll want to share with every lightworker you know.

—**Sammie Fleming,** life coach and sacred circle facilitator

This book is about to ROCK you from the outside in and set your
soul on fire. If you're ready to rock your light, then you've come to
the right place. Tracey Spencer's truth bombs, passion and love for
what she does is captivated in every single word. If you've picked up
this book, your life is about to change for the better. Tracey calls it for
what it is, with her no bullshit approach to life. You're in for a ride, a
badass one with lots of inspiration and love! Enjoy this book, enjoy
the ride and most of all enjoy her passion and love to serve. We all
need a bit of Tracey Spencer in our lives.

—**Heidi Anderson,** broadcaster, writer, speaker, podcaster
- First Time Parents, creator of Shed Your Shit, new mum
and total over-sharer

Rock Your Light is potent, profound and delightfully playful. This book
will build you from the ground up and stoke your inner fire in the best
way possible. Tracey has a way of understanding what you're seeking
before she has even met you, and that level of understanding is rare.
This book is a must have for women ready to arrive and thrive.

—**Tessa Lloyd,** founder of The Art of Insight

Everyone needs someone to believe in their dreams, and Tracey
Spencer has always been that woman for me (and will be for you too)!
Rock Your Light speaks straight to your heart, keeps it real and sets your
soul on fire. Tracey's energy is contagious, and I am grateful to have
her potent words, bound in a book, to pick up and read
whenever I need.

—**Anna Swan,** founder of The Swan Effect

Some books act as a true awakening. This is yours. Designed for the bookshelf of every human that has a knowing it is time to step into their own brilliance and lightwork. Tracey is one of the leading voices of this generation, and she speaks in truth bombs. This book will crack you wide open in the best possible way.

—Ellie Swift, founder of The Swift Marketing Method and Mastermind

Real talk for spiritual entrepreneurs! Tracey Spencer has a way with words that makes you feel like she is speaking directly to your soul. This book is smart, witty, honest and gives practical advice on how to get out of your own way and finish what you started.

—Rosie Rees, founder of Yoni Pleasure Palace and Women's Nude Yoga

Tracey Spencer is the straight-talking spiritual voice that our generation needs. Her just-make-it-happen wisdom has inspired me as a spiritual business person for years, and she's captured the best of it in this book, *Rock Your Light*. Get ready to feel wildly activated after reading it.

—Victoria Bauman, co-founder of The O2 Awakening

Warning – this book may cause you to swap fears, excuses and self-doubt for unshakeable self-belief! Tracey Spencer is an absolute force for Lightworkers who are ready to cut the crap and rock their light more than ever before! *Rock Your Light* will shake you up to just do that, in the best possible, trademark Tracey Spencer way!

—Amanda Hill, women's mentor

Rock Your Light will light a fire under you (lovingly), pushing you in the pursuit of your delicious dreams. For anyone who has ever felt like they want MORE from this life. Trace is a wonderful combination of fire and grace, play and heart, love and power. I was left beaming. I dare you not to go after your dreams after you read this book.

—Julia Hogarth, life coach and meditation teacher of badass, big-hearted women

Rock Your Light is THE book for times to go beyond our limits and into our Lightwork.

Tracey invites us to do this in a playful, potent and powerful way that you can't help but believe and behave that you are meant to be stepping into your purpose, NOW. If you are at the beginning of your awakening and feeling the inklings to share your gifts or have been doing this for a long time and desire for an injection of fresh teachings this book is for you.

Thank you for writing this book and getting it out into the world when us lightworkers need it most.

—Zsuzsa Octaviano, yogi, teacher trainer and women's mentor

Rock Your Light is an invitation, an energetic upgrade, and a crank of the dial for those ready to live the life of their dreams.

In the straight-shooting style she's known and loved for, Tracey Spencer will pluck you swiftly out of doubt and uncertainty, and steer you on bright new path where radical self-belief leads the way.

This refreshingly real book is essential reading for anyone looking to plug in to their full potential — and rock it out.

—Rachel MacDonald, business coach and writer

Compassionate, Fiery and Honest.

Tracey Spencer has this ability to be your wise big sister, your relatable best friend, and your trusty coach all at once – shelling out relatable advice, cheering alongside you as you run your course, reminding you of your brilliance and making you laugh. I didn't take my hand of my heart the whole time I devoured this epic gift to everyone who has ever had even a whisper of a dream to live their lightwork.

Absolute BADASS.

—Jade Baxter, multi-passionate entrepreneur supporting women in magnifying their inner magic

Tracey Spencer is a guiding light and her book *Rock Your Light* is no exception. A pivotal book for our time, inspiring us all to step up, shine our light, lead with heart and to follow our OWN intuition.

—Ruth Balcke, virtual assistant, meditation teacher, lightworker

Wow, this is one of those books you pick up and can't put down. One of those books you notice yourself nodding along to and wishing you had picked up earlier. Tracey Spencer is the wordsmith of our generation. Her words, energy and lessons will change your life. This I know first-hand from working with Tracey and reading *Rock Your Light*.

Tracey Spencer is the real deal and will deliver you exactly what you need to rock your lightwork. This book is full of powerful energy, ah-ha moments, a kick up the bum and the mindset shifts you need.

—Daisy Moore, life and business coach,
founder of daisymoore.co.nz

ROCK YOUR LIGHT

LESSONS FOR LIGHTWORKERS

AND SPIRITUAL STRAIGHT TALK

TO MAKE SHIT HAPPEN

TRACEY SPENCER

ROCK YOUR LIGHT

LESSONS FOR LIGHTWORKERS
AND SPIRITUAL STRAIGHT TALK
TO MAKE SHIT HAPPEN

the kind press

Cover and interior design by Elle Lynn

Cataloguing-in-Publication entry is available from the National Library Australia.

NATIONAL
LIBRARY
OF AUSTRALIA

ISBN 978-0-6487927-1-0 (Paperback)

ISBN 978-0-6487927-2-7 (eBook)

This book is written for lightworkers everywhere who are showing up and shining bright.

Please. Never. Ever. Stop.

CONTENTS

PART ONE
PURPOSE

PART TWO

POWER

PART THREE

PROSPERITY

YOU DON'T
<u>OUTSHINE OTHERS,</u>
YOU SHINE
for OTHERS.

AN ODE TO
LIGHTWORKERS

We are to be the ascended masters of our times.
We are the next generation of lightworkers emerging.
And you reading this,
Are one of them.

I know you have a big vision on your heart,
And even bigger self-doubt sitting next to it.
I want to remind you that you don't need to subscribe to struggle anymore,
Instead, you can thrive on creative expression,
And living abundantly from your heart.

We each have a deep inner calling to serve,
We're each on a soul mission, driven by our intuition.
Keep choosing your internal alignment over external validation,
It's not going to make sense to everyone, and it doesn't need to,
Your only job is to keep following your inner whispers.

Your presence speaks before you even open your mouth,
Your heart is the qualification you need for this work.
You've already been doing it for lifetimes, trust me.
Let your fears fade into background noise,
As courage takes the steering wheel from now on.

Age-old teachings are to be delivered in a fun, fresh new way,
A way that vibrates truth at the heart level,
Reminding us that we are perfect as we are,
And the more fun we can have along the way,
The better.

It's time to re-define purpose and power,
Without the energetic baggage from our parents,
Weighing us down and keeping us stuck for another five lifetimes,
It's not ours to carry anymore.
Let it be lighter and brighter than ever before.

Activate your radiance,
Don't run from it.
Believe in yourself more than anything,
You are more ready than you think you are,
Keep showing up one step at a time, you've got this.

I promise you won't outshine others,
But you will be called on to shine for them.
We need you now more than ever,
To rock your light,
And to never, ever dim it down again.

LIGHTWORKER

definition

A lightworker is called to share their light and gifts to help make a positive impact on the world. A lightworker is highly intuitive, knowing they are here for something special. A lightworker can intuit what others think, feel or need, they are here to be of service, as a beacon for the Earth, and commit to healing humanity. A lightworker devotes to sharing their light and positive energy with the world wherever they go and with whatever they do. Stepping into your power as a lightworker is about following the call of your heart to create a life that feels so lit up, that you light others up too.

INTRODUCTION

When I was twenty years old, life began to feel off. I was doing all the typical things I thought I *should* be doing at that age—going to university, partying it up with friends on weekends, and living a carefree life. But for some reason, I saw cracks appearing in the life I'd convinced myself I'd wanted.

I can recall the exact moment when I heard my intuition for the first time. It was a Thursday morning. I was in my room at uni, hungover, sitting in a body—my body—a body I no longer recognised because of the college-binge-drinking lifestyle I'd fallen into. And I was about to spiral into more negative self-critical thoughts. In short, I felt like shit. I remember thinking, *this wasn't what I signed up for, how the heck did I end up here?* Everything from the outside seemed to be ticking along okay, but I wasn't feeling the way I thought I was going to feel on the inside. There was a misalignment and my soul was starting to speak up about it because *She* had had enough. For the first time, I was truly ready to listen. I sat up in my bed, closed my eyes and heard the words: *Do you really think this is the best you've got, Trace? This isn't your path. You are here to teach, speak and help inspire others.* I didn't just hear these words that day; I felt them.

Teach? Speak? Inspire others? What the heck about? was my first thought.

This wasn't exactly the sea parting lightbulb moment I wanted heading into my end of semester exams. However, I was getting the message loud and clear. That semester break I deferred—read: left with no intention to return to my degree and went travelling overseas. I came back with a clear intention to take better care of myself, and to figure out what the heck I was going to do next.

That was eight years ago. I've been on an inner journey of awakening ever since. It started with reading every self-help book I could get my hands on, attending self-love and meditation workshops, and studying the Law of Attraction. I wrote pages and pages of gratitude notes in my journal, hours of Googling chakras, and pretty much soaking up the wisdom of any spiritual lectures I could find online. As my inner world started to come alive, so did my outer world. Instead of walking in at sunrise on a Sunday morning, heels in hand from a big night out, I was rolling out my yoga mat ready to tune in. Instead of getting drunk every Friday night, I was in bed watching Gabrielle Bernstein lectures on YouTube and soaking up the potent words of Rebecca Campbell. And instead of saying 'yes' to everything to fit in, I started saying 'no' to anything that was no longer lighting me up.

For months, even years, I was the girl at the back of the yoga class and self-love workshop crying and wanting to understand why I always felt like something was missing in my life. I might have seemed confident at the time, but on the inside, I was lost. I felt disconnected, confused, insecure and wondered how I was ever going to feel better. Even though I caught glimpses of myself teaching, speaking and even writing this book, these big dreams came with an even bigger self-doubt sitting right next to them. I never knew how I was going to make things happen and create the life I really wanted. Especially when my current reality looked nothing like the one that would make me cry with *joy* in morning meditations.

The thing that was *missing* was *me*.

Through my awakening journey, I had people around me telling me 'I'd changed'. I knew it wasn't true. I didn't change. I just became more of my true self. And little by little, my light turned back on, and before too long I made it my mission to help awaken the light in others. You might be at a point in your life where things you used to like don't really light you up anymore. Perhaps the uni degree isn't really what you want to be doing, or the job you've been working at for years is leaving you bored and creatively dry. You may suddenly stop eating foods that don't feel right for your body, or you may become increasingly sensitive to certain environments. You might even see colours in your meditations and feel your hands tingle with warmth as you think about your dreams. Even your emotions might feel like a rollercoaster some days, and you go from feeling flat with no energy to crying with an overwhelming sense of gratitude.

Are you starting to become the person who people refer to as 'the positive-hippie-one'? It feels like something has changed even if you can't exactly put your finger on it, but you know you can never go back. Maybe you're noticing synchronicities around you as if the Universe is trying to tell you things and lead you in a new direction? And finally, you're sitting up and paying attention. Just like me, you want to get high on gratitude and not gossip anymore. You crave soul family with real connection, not just superficial conversations and the same old shit. You feel you are outgrowing certain people in your life. And you have a big dream pulling on your heart, but you don't know where or how to start because none of your friends really *get it*.

Whether you have been on an inner journey for a while now or not, this book has landed in your hands for a reason. You're ready for more. My intention for this book is to remind you that your dreams aren't fluffy or fake or some random nonsense you made up for attention. They are real, ripe and ready for you to bring them into the world. It's time for us to commit to living a life where we choose internal alignment over external validation every day. It's time to stop doubting ourselves and letting fear run our lives. You have a divine responsibility to show up and take action on the great work you are here to do. There are people out there who are waiting for your light to help guide them home to theirs.

It's time for you to step boldly into a life of greater ***purpose, power*** and ***prosperity*** that comes from having the courage to follow the calling in your heart.

YOU'RE A
lightworker.
AND YOU'VE GOT
WORK TO DO.

PART ONE

PURPOSE

LESSON 1

YOUR PATTERNS LEAD YOU TO YOUR PURPOSE

Over the last few years, I have had conversations with hundreds of women who constantly feel overwhelmed at the thought of trying to figure out what their life purpose is. When they see other people on social media who have found their soul calling, they start comparing themselves. They question if they have anything to offer or if other people have something special that they don't have. My hope is that you look at your purpose in a different way and see it has been weaving its way through your life experiences all along. You are much closer than you think.

Ever since I was young, I wanted to be a teacher. I always felt a strong inner desire to teach in some way, but I could never imagine myself teaching in a school, which you can imagine left me quite confused. If I didn't want to work in a school, then how was I ever going to be a teacher? *Well, I love learning about the human body, and I'm great at human biology, so I guess I will teach that?* I thought, as I enrolled in a university degree.

The thing that trips most people up from finding their purpose is that they feel embarrassed when they move through different courses, or careers. That's because they still haven't found the thing that truly lights them up. I believe it's never about going searching for your purpose, and that your purpose naturally starts to awaken the more that you awaken parts of yourself that you have been shutting down. Each of us has been given clues and shown signs of our purpose through life experiences when we have felt most lit up. We just don't know it at the time because we are too busy looking at what everyone else is doing.

When I look back on my high school days, I can see where the Universe was gifting me practice runs in my purpose. I was always placed in a leadership position where I would have to speak in front of people. I'd offer words of encouragement to my peers and be responsible for bringing people together and making them feel part of a team. I was the head girl of my primary school, a house captain at high school and often sports captain. Being in these leadership roles early on gave me many opportunities to practice speaking in front of groups of people before truly realising what the Universe was preparing me for. Bringing groups of people together to play sport later manifested into bringing groups of people together for spiritual awakenings. I look back and see I had been unofficially coaching, teaching, and leading for years, which would later become the foundations of my career.

Public speaking has always magically weaved its way into my life. I loved giving presentations in English while most of my friends would be plotting their escape plan. Of course, I would get nervous and feel a rush of energy beforehand, but I always felt that speaking was something I was here to do. And this was just a warm-up for what was to come. When I was growing up, I made my parents buy me a microphone so I could record myself on a tape recorder as if I were a radio host pretending to interview people. Little did I know at the time, this was me practicing for a podcast I would create and host in the future. It also made me comfortable holding a microphone whilst on stage at large speaking events.

On a recent visit to my family home, I found my primary school portfolios that I hadn't seen in years. As I flicked through them, I noticed my top marks were always in creative writing. For some reason, it just came naturally to me. My imagination would take my writing hand on an adventure across the page as I would pen stories and poems. I still remember sitting in my year 12 English exam where I was writing a speech for the creative section. I thought my teachers would either love it or think I was completely crazy. I had no idea where the idea had come from, but I went with it. I later received top marks of my class for that piece, so apparently creative writing was one of my gifts back then, one day leading me to write this book.

Living your purpose is one of the most natural things that you can do in this lifetime. The thing that confuses most people about their purpose is that they don't feel that what comes naturally to them is a big enough deal. We tend to believe our purpose needs to feel like a big deal or that it should be hard in order to be powerful. They think if everyone can do it, or if it's easy, it's not worthy. They forget they have natural gifts that other people don't and vice versa. One thing I really want you to know is that just because something comes easily to you, does *not* mean that it isn't powerful and needed. It's up to each of us to own the unique gifts we've been given and share them with the world.

I encourage you to look back on the parts of your life when you have felt most connected to yourself and where things flowed and came naturally to you.

Rock Your Light Reflection

WHAT HAVE YOU ALWAYS FOUND YOURSELF COMING BACK TO?

WHAT BRINGS YOU THE GREATEST JOY, AND WHICH SAME PATTERNS HAVE BEEN PLAYING OUT AND MANIFESTING IN YOUR LIFE UP UNTIL NOW?

THESE ARE CLUES.

Chances are you've been doing your lightwork all along, you just didn't realise it at the time.

THE UNIVERSE
IS ALWAYS GIFTING YOU
PRACTICE RUNS
IN YOUR PURPOSE,

pay attention.

LESSON 2

DO THE DRAFT COPY

If I could gift everyone who is chasing their dreams, or just starting out on their journey, one piece of advice it would be this. Be in the energy of what you want to create before it is created. I like to call this *doing the draft copy*. The sooner you can be in the draft copy version of your highest vision, the better. I often ask my clients who are ready to step into their power as leaders and teachers, 'Okay, so, what would be the easiest next step to get you into your teaching energy? What's the first draft copy version of your dreams . . . the blog, the book, the business, the website, the workshop, the podcast, the event? Let's start there.'

What I want you to understand is that when you see a vision of your dreams, the vision is being presented to you in its full final copy version. Whether it's catching glimpses of yourself speaking on stage, starting a business, bringing people together, winning an award, helping others heal, writing a book, or whatever it may be. It's being shown to you in its fullest expression so you can see the end vision of what's possible for you.

This is where people get stuck because the end vision often feels so far away from your current reality, so it feels impossible to even take the first step. Most people get so overwhelmed about how they will do step 10 before they've even looked at what the first step requires. We get all caught up in our mind on the parts that aren't even a big deal, and we try to answer all the questions we don't need to know the answers to just yet. This is merely a distraction from your ego trying to keep you procrastinating for another six months, until you have all your ducks lined up. Or until the timing is better, or until you 'know enough' to teach it. I bet you've heard those same stories a few times before, too. You can believe all the stories and excuses in the world about why you can't do something, why it's easy for some people, but not you, why you don't have enough time or money... the list goes on. You can keep hanging out with your excuses, or you can get to work creating the draft copy of something epic now.

This book has been guiding me for years. One morning the vision of this book came clear and fast out of nowhere, like a jolt of energy that made me sit up and pay full attention. Instantly, I could see the yoga studios I would host book tours at. I could see women reading and scribbling notes on the pages. I saw a beautiful community that would come together to learn and grow from this book. I remember getting an intuitive hit that I needed to spread these lessons through teaching a *Rock Your Light Masterclass* across Australia. In my Melbourne masterclass, I said to everyone at the end, 'In a few years, I will be back teaching here again and I will have a book in my hand.' I said it with such conviction and certainty because I knew with every bone in my body that it was true, even though it still felt so far away. I was already in the practice run of my book tour before I'd written the book. I was teaching the lessons I was going to write. I was hiring the venues I knew I wanted to host book launches at. I was sharing these lessons on social media and learning new marketing skills I knew I would need to use in the future to help spread the message of my book. I was doing all the things I would do with the book in my hand, before I actually had the book in my hand. I was committed to nailing the draft copy, knowing that the real deal would soon follow.

A similar thing happened before I became a kundalini yoga teacher. I was a student who felt like they had just landed on the missing piece. None of my friends had heard of this powerful practice before. It was hard for me to find classes in my local community after one of my favourite teachers took a break from teaching. I remember thinking, *who is going to teach this to young people in my area if I don't?* I was only a few months into running my coaching business when I started leading small sister circles on a Friday night at a local yoga studio, another draft copy of my vision that later became a booked-out women's workshop. Each time I would share one of the kundalini yoga meditations I had been practicing and teach the mantra or breath technique to the women who attended. Even if I looked a little weird whilst doing it, I didn't care because I knew I had to share these powerful tools that were helping me transform from within.

I look back now and celebrate my courage to teach before I was ready, before I had the perfect meditation voice or before I really knew what I was doing. I was probably teaching it wrong half the time, but my passion and enthusiasm to serve and share the teachings was enough. I didn't need to know everything. I just knew I needed to start. I never intended on becoming a kundalini yoga teacher until I received clear guidance before bed one night, saying,

'It's time to teach kundalini yoga.' *I guess I should become a teacher then,* I thought. And so, I did. More on that story later in the book.

Do you have a vision that's hot on your heart and bursting to be created but you are constantly overthinking it and trying to be perfect before you put it out to the world? Then I invite you to write out a draft copy version. Anything is better than nothing. Once you get energy moving on the first copy, you'll be surprised how quickly things flow.

I feel this book is still the draft copy of a greater vision that I can't see yet. But it's not my job to know exactly how it's going to look now. It's my job to get to work on doing the draft copy and sharing my gifts and voice with the world. Remember, draft 2 can only become clearer once you've shown up fully for draft 1.

The blog is the draft copy of the book.
The Instagram story is the draft copy of the speaking gig.
The 1:1 mentoring session is the draft copy of the mastermind groups.
The sister circle is the draft copy of the 6-week online course.
The weekend workshop is the draft copy of the week-long retreat.

✦ Rock Your Light Reflection

WHAT IS YOUR VISION FOR YOUR NEXT BUSINESS, BOOK, OR
CREATIVE PROJECT?

WRITE DOWN 10 DRAFT COPIES THAT YOU CAN DO TO BE IN THE
ENERGY OF THE FINAL VISION, BEFORE THE FINAL VISION HAS FULLY
MANIFESTED.

IF THERE WERE 10 VERSIONS OF THIS VISION THAT YOU COULD
CREATE AND PRACTICE ALONG THE WAY TO THE FINAL COPY,
WHAT WOULD THEY LOOK LIKE?
HOW WOULD YOU DO THE FIRST ONE NOW?

YOUR <u>DRAFT COPY</u> IS
PERFECT
FOR NOW,
STOP *judging* IT
AND START *living* IT.

LESSON 3

GO FOR YOUR GOLD MEDAL VISION

People often ask me how I got started with my business and how I have been so driven to serve in the ways I have. The truth is, I just decided to go for it. I look back and thank my younger self who hit publish on her first ever blog post without truly understanding what blogging really was or how to properly do it. I didn't care how many people would read it. I just knew I had to write and do something to move this energy and passion in my heart.

From starting and fumbling my way around that first blog whilst I was still working as a personal trainer, I connected with a new vision. I felt different, like a new energy was moving through me. One day whilst working at the gym it came to me. *This isn't it yet, there are other ways I want to use my gifts.* After surrendering what this 'other way' might look like, I randomly landed on a life coaching website. Life coaching was still quite new in Australia back then, so I didn't truly know what exactly it was. However, after reading this particular website I just knew I had to do it and enrolled in the course that same day. I know that something bigger guided me to that website.

It's funny when you find yourself in a course where you expect to be learning new skills, but you feel like they have been there all along. They were simply just waiting to be remembered and reawakened. So, here I found myself fresh out of a coaching course and still trying to decide what my main message and mission would be. For many lightworkers, this is where we get way too up in our heads trying to nail our niche or have the perfect elevator pitch before we can put ourselves and our work out into the world to serve.

When I graduated as a coach, I was still in the fitness industry and had just started a wellness business with a good friend. I remember getting to a point where something just wasn't feeling right, and it felt as if the Universe was tugging me in two different directions. We would be planning our next event and I would be daydreaming of being on stage dropping spiritual straight talk. I was so confused because I absolutely loved what I was doing, but I could also feel I was being pulled in a new direction.

One of my best friends, Hellè asked me a question that changed everything for me. I had been explaining to her how I was being tugged in two directions, both of which were great. I'd been trying to decide which would be the 'smarter, more logical' path because I knew they both had so much potential. I had seen many others be successful in these directions.

She asked me to close my eyes and imagine a podium in front of me, just like they have at the Olympics with a step for bronze, silver and gold placings. She then asked me to imagine that my life had three paths, or three options to what I could drive my energy towards creating.

"Tell me about your bronze vision, the one you know is pretty good and would tick all the right boxes on paper."

I replied, "Staying in the fitness industry, being a personal trainer and maybe going to study something else."

"OK, good. Now tell me about the next two, what's your silver and what's your gold?"

I was silent for a while as she cued me to close my eyes and really see the vision in my heart of who I was truly here to be. Not the version of me that I thought I should be. I eventually admitted to myself that I had been trying to convince myself I wanted a certain path because I knew the success it had brought to other people around me. I wanted so badly for it to be my potential and my vision too, but the truth in my heart was that I didn't want it. My ego did, but my heart didn't. We can't settle for Plan B in the fear that Plan A won't manifest.

I looked at her with misty eyes and said, "I want to be an author, speaker and spiritual teacher. I don't care how long it takes or how many people judge me. This is my soul work. I don't really know how it's going to look or how I'm going to make money from it, but I know that I can't not do it."

From that day forward opportunities to teach, speak and write would show up and almost land in my lap. It's like the Universe was responding to me by saying, 'Finally you are paying attention, now let's get to work.'

Anytime I experience fear or self-doubt coming up distracting me from my mission or if something feels stretchy, I always ask myself this question. 'Is this moving me closer to my gold medal vision, or keeping me from it?' I encourage you to ask yourself the same question right now with anything you are trying to make a clear decision on. Is it guiding you closer to your highest potential? If so, say yes and go for gold.

Rock Your Light Reflection

IF YOU ARE CURRENTLY BEING PULLED IN DIFFERENT DIRECTIONS
AND DON'T KNOW WHAT THE RIGHT OPTION IS FOR YOU, I
ENCOURAGE YOU TO PUT THE PROS AND CONS LISTS ASIDE AND ASK
YOURSELF; IS THIS MOVING ME CLOSER TO MY HIGHEST POTENTIAL,
MY GOLD MEDAL VISION, OR KEEPING ME FROM IT?

Go for gold, always!

THE 'SHOULDS' WILL
NEVER FULLY
SATISFY YOUR SOUL.

LESSON 4

LET YOUR VISION LEAD YOU

When you allow yourself to turn down the negative voice in your head enough to really tune in, there is always a subtle pull of energy trying to lead you to the next step on your path. The problem is we don't give ourselves the time and space to truly listen. Or we hear the answer and it's not logical, so we instantly shut it down and shrug it off as a silly idea. We focus our energy on things we think we should be doing according to what we see in everyone else's journey rather than tuning in to the truth of our own soul.

We can become so distracted and waste our creative energy on convincing ourselves we want other people's lives from social media. In truth, our mission should be to create and love our own beautiful life, our way. There is a reason your heart's vision and potential doesn't look like anybody else's, and that's because it isn't meant to.

Years ago, when my vision guided me to become a kundalini yoga teacher, it made no logical sense to me. I was fresh out of graduating as a life coach, lying in bed one night thinking, *what's next, where do I need to go?* I wasn't really expecting a response when instantly,

I could hear the words, 'It's time to teach kundalini yoga,' very clearly as though Yogi Bhajan himself was in the room talking to me. My immediate response was to give the Universe the bird and a list of ten reasons why I couldn't do it. Why I wasn't ready. Why people would think I'm weird if all of a sudden, I was rocking a turban and chanting mantras. And my question to the Universe was around how the heck I was going to pay for the training. *How dare you!* I thought.

Next thing I knew I was Googling teacher trainings and landed on one that sent shivers up my spine. I'd found my teacher on the other side of Australia. The next training was a year away, and that didn't excite my impatient tendencies whatsoever. I kept searching to find a training a month away in my local area. I tried to convince myself it would be more convenient, but something didn't feel right with that training either. So, I let it go. Shrugged it off and decided on neither.

The following night the same thing happened.
It's time to teach Kundalini Yoga, followed by *Check the website again.* So I did. A new training date was beginning in twelve weeks. All I needed was a $500 deposit, and I was in. At the time, my lack of savings was giving me anxiety and so was the voice in my head saying, *And how do you think you're going to afford this training; you should be saving? You just became a coach; do you think it's smart to start another course?* I didn't know how, but I knew I had to figure it out.

      I entered my card details.

      Deposit paid. I was in.

My vision was leading me, and my only job was to take my hands off the steering wheel, show up and trust it would support me.

I listened. I took the leap. Two weeks later, I won an Emerging Coach of the Year award in which the cash prize was $500. Turns out the Universe did have my back, especially because I was willing to listen and show up no matter what. I wasn't just asking for the guidance; I was acting on it. To this day, I still don't know how I paid for that course. But I did. It turned out to be one of the best things I ever did and was a large piece of the puzzle in being here writing this book. I'm so glad I got out of the way and let my vision lead the way and work its magic through me.

Rock Your Light Reflection

WHERE AM I LETTING MY FEAR OF NOT KNOWING EXACTLY HOW SOMETHING WILL TURN OUT, STOP ME FROM SHOWING UP AND TAKING THE FIRST STEP?

The Universe has a plan far better than yours, be willing to get your humanness out of the way and just go for it!

23

GO BIG

AND THE UNIVERSE WILL

GO *bigger.*

LESSON 5

SHOW UP AND YOU WILL BE SHOWN

When I began my inner journey, it was for me. Not for anyone else. I just wanted to feel better within myself. I wanted to know who I truly was, what I was here for and what was possible for me in this lifetime. But never in my wildest dreams did I think my life would turn out how it has. I was so lost at that point in my life that all I did was follow my intuition each day and show up to what *it* was asking of me. Even when *it* didn't make sense. Day by day I strengthened the connection to my inner voice and to the Universe. I followed the signs and listened to the nudges guiding me towards different books, courses, podcasts, workshops and the perfectly timed teachers I needed to help me along the way. All along the Universe was guiding me to the experiences and lessons that I was going to teach and write about in the future. I just never knew it at the time.

It's important to remember that your path of awakening and heal-ing is not going to be linear. It's messy and all over the place, but it's also going to be perfect for you. You will feel like you nail something and then it flares up in your face again. It can feel like three steps forward and two back at times, just keep going. As lightworkers in these times, we have to remember that we signed up for this work. We signed up to master certain lessons, so that we could hold space to share them and inspire others into a new way of thinking and living. We signed up to expand our consciousness and help elevate the consciousness in others, no matter how long it takes. If you are feeling the call to step up and serve other people and help them heal in some way, I guarantee your ego is going to instantly come firing at you with thoughts like: *Yeah, well who do you think you are to teach that? Who is going to listen to you? That's just fluffy stuff, no one will understand it so don't bother.*

You know that vision you have of you teaching, writing, speaking, healing, leading, creating, serving and bringing people together? The one that covers you in goosebumps and makes your hands and heart tingle whenever you think about it? It isn't fluffy or fake like your ego will try to convince you it is. That vision is real, ripe and ready for you to pay more attention to it. It is choosing you and it's your job now to do whatever you can to get moving with it. You wouldn't have been shown it if you weren't ready to own it.

You have everything you need right now to take your next step, which is exactly why it is being presented to you. Let me remind you that you would not have been shown it if you weren't ready to own it. You aren't receiving the 3am downloads, the inspiration, the excitement, and all the perfectly timed synchronicities for nothing. Maybe you have been thinking about running a certain workshop, and then you overhear someone at the supermarket talking about the exact topic you want to teach. Or someone hands you a book or shares a post with you they saw on social media saying, 'Hey, I thought of you.' This is the Universe saying it's *go*-time!

I wasn't shown the book vision until I had showed up for the blog. I wasn't shown the speaking opportunities until I pressed record on my first vlogs. I wasn't shown the vision of my online programs until I showed up to teach self-love to four women on my lounge-room floor on a Sunday morning five years ago.

Here's where I give you a short and sweet pep-talk. The Universe can't and won't pour in fresh energy and new ideas if you aren't taking serious action on what is already being offered to you. Know that it isn't your job to know every single detailed step about how things will turn out. Your job is to be in the joy of your lightwork and be willing to show up, and then be shown time and time again. Your next step is right there, and it's time to say yes to it.
You have everything you need for the next step.
Just say 'yes' and show up.

Rock Your Light Reflection

WHAT VISION IN YOUR HEART IS REQUIRING YOU TO TRUST RIGHT NOW INSTEAD OF NEEDING TO KNOW WHAT EVERY SINGLE DETAIL WILL LOOK LIKE BEFORE YOU SHOW UP AND SAY 'YES'?

WHAT IF YOU SHOWED UP KNOWING YOU WILL BE SHOWN EXACTLY WHAT YOU NEED, AT THE EXACT MOMENT YOU ARE READY TO RECEIVE IT?

Stop doubting your downloads.
They are ripe and ready, and so are you.

YOU WOULDN'T HAVE
BEEN SHOWN IT
IF YOU WEREN'T
READY TO <u>OWN IT.</u>

LESSON 6

GET OUT OF YOUR HEAD AND ON WITH YOUR MISSION

For most lightworkers creative ideas and inspiration never seems to be the issue keeping us stuck. We are tapped in and connected to a cosmic highway in which there is no lack of ideas or creative possibilities, so inspiration isn't ever the problem. The issue is always found in the overwhelm that we face looking at the distance and time it may take us to get there. Lack of time is another classic excuse from your ego keeping you from taking aligned action towards your dreams, yet it is very rarely the truth. Overthinking, fear-based laziness and procrastination are the issues that are really keeping us from getting out there and making shit happen.

I bet you get revved up and excited when you sit with the energy of your dreams. Then you write it all down in your journal, quickly and easily mapping out exactly how you see it unfolding. Then as soon as you give yourself too much breathing space between idea and action, you get caught up in your head, overthinking all the little details that don't really even matter. Procrastination is just perfectionism in disguise, like an evil twin sister.

It's easy to freak out thinking about how far away your dreams still feel from your current reality and usually your current bank balance. You are being shown the result of a vision because the Universe wants to give you a preview of what is possible. This vision and dream will perfectly manifest in weeks, months or years, exactly as it should. But remember, you aren't meant to go from zero to hero on your vision in one day like your ego thinks you should. It's not all meant to happen *all* at once. You are being given the completed outline to join the dots together, and without the Universe dangling the carrot, you wouldn't know where to start chomping.

When I first started connecting to the energy of this book, of course, it scared the heck out of me. It felt like such a faraway, impossible goal to reach. As soon as numbers and deadlines started playing a part, I became really overwhelmed—30,000 words sounded like a lot. Especially on days where I stared at a blinking cursor for hours wondering if I had anything of value to share. I wondered how I was going to be the one to bring these words to life when I had never written a book before.

On particularly overwhelming days where it felt like I was never going to get the book done, I keep holding the vision of the finished book. I knew all I had to do each day was get out of my head, show up and start writing. Some days I could only write a few dot points, other days 2,000 words would fly out without me even thinking twice about them. Some days all I could manage was to text a friend: 'I can't wait to share this book with you.'

I had to keep moving with the energy even on the days it felt like nothing was happening. I knew it was all part of the process. Don't let yourself become stuck in overwhelm by putting all your energy into the big picture, just take the first step. Any time I would think too much about the book and about the word count, I would get into my head and out of my creative flow. I stopped focusing on writing a book and focused on writing one lesson at a time. Turns out a bunch of lessons put together in one place was all I needed for the book.

In the moments you still feel really far away from your dreams, remind yourself that right now you are actually the closest you've ever been. Know that taking a single step is better than all the steps you're thinking of taking but procrastinating on. Your main goal isn't to get it perfect from day one, it's to always keep energy moving toward your dreams, no matter what.

Rock Your Light Reflection

DO YOU CONSTANTLY OVERTHINK THINGS?

ARE YOU STRUGGLING TO GET OUT OF YOUR HEAD?

IF THIS IS YOU, HEAD OVER TO WWW.ROCKYOURLIGHT.COM.AU AND LET THE BREATH OF FIRE BECOME YOUR NEW BEST FRIEND!

> **As Yogi Bhajan says,**
> **"When the time is on you, start,**
> **and the pressure will be off."**

YOUR PURPOSE IS

unfolding

PERFECTLY FOR YOU.

LESSON 7

FOCUS ON THE RIPPLES, NOT THE RANKS

It is such a privilege and an honour to do your lightwork in this lifetime and to help inspire—even just one person—and make positive changes in people's lives. We get so caught up in the numbers game thinking we aren't *making* a difference or *doing* enough until we have a million followers and a million dollars to match it.

I often think about one of my mentors who I've worked with for seven years now. I think about the day I walked into his office feeling lost, confused, and disconnected. I knew I had more to give to the world, but I had no idea how the heck I was even going to even start to feel better. Whenever I get up in my head about the numbers, I think of the impact he has had on my life. How easily he could have said, 'Oh, it's only Trace, it's only one person, so what's the point? It probably won't even help.' If he had thought that then you would not be reading this book. Remember that you too are one person. Imagine if the person you looked to for support didn't bother because they thought 'it's only one person what's the point', how would you feel? We are always chasing more and forgetting to celebrate the great work we are doing. That's because the mind will keep you from your power in the present moment by convincing you it doesn't count until you're getting paid more, or you have more followers, or all your events are booked out. We need to stop being stuck focusing on the likes, instead of the actual lightwork.

I bet you don't allow yourself to celebrate the three people coming to your workshop because you're convincing yourself that it doesn't count until it's fifty people. You don't allow yourself to feel really proud of the amazing coaching session you just had with your first pro bono client. That's because your ego comes flying in to take the mic and says, 'Yeah, but you didn't get paid for it, so it doesn't even count yet.' I want to give you a huge heart to heart reminder: it counts—all of it.

Have big goals to reach for, but not to the detriment of celebrating the way you're courageously showing up right now, as you are.

If there was one piece of advice to add here on how to stay anchored in your lightwork and expand your impact, it would be to bring your full heart and energy wherever you teach. Whether you are speaking to five people or five thousand people, bring your full heart no matter what because people will feel it. You won't have more people show up for your work until you show up fully to serve the people right in front of you putting their hand up for help. I have always made this commitment to myself—whenever I am in front of people and gifted and opportunity to serve. I show up fully, no matter how many people there are in that moment to receive it because you just never know the impact you can have on someone. Don't let your ego distract you into being too busy doing a headcount or worrying how many likes your event photos will get on social media. Focus on a heartcount, not a headcount. Remember the one by one by one rule.

> One open heart at a time.
> One expanded consciousness at a time.
> One loving thought at a time.
> One empowered decision at a time.
> One awakening at a time.
> One meditation at a time.
> One step forward at a time.
> One outpour of self-belief at a time.
> One.

You are impacting more people than you will ever know. There is a golden thread of light weaving its way through you when you show up to serve no matter what the outcome. People aren't just seeing, they are feeling. They are paying more attention than you think, and most of the time they might not want to admit it, and that's okay. Even if they don't 'like, comment or share' your work, can you just trust that it's being felt?

One Sunday morning at our local Farmers Markets, Luke and I passed two older ladies and their grandchildren picking up rubbish. I stopped to thank them. They weren't there for the applause or recognition. They weren't doing it to get Instagram likes. 'That is lightwork,' I said to Luke. They were doing it because that is what lightworkers do. They show up to help no matter what.

Believe me when I say that your presence is impacting people who you will probably never even meet. People are receiving from your presence every single day. Think about how many people have impacted your life who will never know that they have. We don't write to every author of every book that's changed or impacted our lives. But they have shown up in your life, and they keep showing up because that is what they are put on this planet to do. Now it's time for you to do the same.

**One by
one by
one.**

BE IN YOUR
LIGHTWORK FOR LIFE,
NOT JUST FOR THE LIKES.

LESSON 8

NOT EVERYBODY IS GOING TO GET IT

It breaks my heart when lightworkers give up on their dreams the second someone doubts or questions them. Not everybody is going to get it. And here's the thing, they are not meant to.

It can be disheartening when you start your awakening journey and you begin to feel lit up about everything you are learning—excitedly, you just want to shout it from the rooftops and tell every single person you know—only to be shut down with eye rolls and a not-so-subtle indication you've lost your marbles. Let me clear the air and tell you that your family, and possibly most of your friends, won't *get it*. They won't understand the undeniable pull on your heart to change direction and listen to an inner voice over the voice of society. Nor will they get that you are making big decisions with the only explanation to them being 'it just feels right'. They won't get it when being hungover every weekend isn't really your idea of living your best life anymore. They won't get it when you quit your job with no real back-up plan, but you just trust it's going to work out. And they won't get it when you're pouring your life savings into your personal development and new business venture rather than settling down and buying a house. They won't get it, but you *will*.

This time is an important part of your journey where I encourage you to turn your gaze inwards and get to know yourself on a deeper level. Read the book, go to the workshops, sit in stillness, try new hobbies, grow yourself, hire a coach to support you in getting to know the real you. The real you that is sick of hiding and is now wanting to emerge into the world and call in your own new community of like-minded friends to support you on your journey.

Here's where I want to let you know that there will probably be a time on your journey where you feel isolated. I call this transition time 'the gap'. I know from experience that the gap can feel really scary and confusing. It can make you question if you are making the right decision or if you are making everything up. If you are truly built for living your dreams or if you are ever going to find people who love the same things that you love. Just know that you're in a magical transition period. Let go of the old and create space —allowing the Universe to reorganise certain environments and relationships in your life to align you more with your higher self. This is happening for your highest good, even in the moments it feels like your whole life has been thrown into a washing machine. Trust it.

When you truly start being yourself, you will attract people who bring out more of your truth. It is absolutely crucial you surround yourself with people who see the world in a similar way you do so you can build a bulletproof belief in yourself and in your lightwork. If you are constantly surrounded by people who question you and laugh at your dreams, then you will always have an undercurrent of self-doubt holding you back. That's because you don't believe people will ever take you seriously.

Please stop trying to impress people who don't really value and see the real you. Stop trying to pull people out of the mud who don't want to be pulled out. It will become an exhausting and never-ending uphill battle in which you are always feeling like you need to prove yourself. It's tiring and unnecessary. Your job is to plant seeds wherever you go but stay focused on charging forward with the people who are moving in the same direction as you.

Rock Your Light Reflection

ARE PEOPLE NOT READY TO RECEIVE WHAT YOU HAVE TO SAY?

OR ARE YOU JUST NOT READY TO FULLY OWN IT?

Your community can't find you, until you've truly found yourself.

PEOPLE WILL <u>STOP</u>
questioning YOU
WHEN YOU <u>STOP</u>
questioning YOURSELF.

LESSON 9

TAKE YOUR PURPOSE OFF A PEDASTAL

Take your purpose off a pedestal. And while you're at it, take everyone else's off one too.

The easiest way to keep your dreams far away from you is to put a ridiculous amount of energetic charge and pressure on them to be perfect from the get-go. The more you charge your dreams up to be a huge big deal, the further away they will feel, like a huge unattainable mountain in the distance.

What if I told you that living your lightwork could actually be fun? And that you don't have to take it so seriously and put a ridiculous amount of pressure on yourself to look a certain way or get it right all the time. And I say this as a type-A personality who often places tonnes of unnecessary pressure on myself! I know the feeling of having big dreams can feel bigger than you, but it's only your mind that is blowing it up to feel that way. The truth is that living your highest purpose isn't just your dream, it's the Universe's dream for you too. You came in perfectly programmed to carry out your highest vision. You've just got to shake off some pressure and rock it your way.

A highly creative and intuitive friend of mine has been working as a hairdresser for many years. I remember having a conversation with her when she was feeling like she wasn't in her true purpose. Stuck in a loop of comparison, she felt her work wasn't really making a difference like the other people who she admired and looked up to. She loved hairdressing, but decided she wanted to expand her toolkit and enrolled to study life coaching. She had many friends and coaches around her who she aspired to be like and was feeling a constant inner tug-of-war that her purpose wasn't 'spiritual enough'.

When I was recently getting my hair done, I overheard one of her clients say this.
'When you were massaging my head, I felt tingles all the way to my fingertips, it felt like I was receiving a healing. Thank you so much for making my day.'
I could tell she was getting the message from the Universe that she was more in her purpose than she thought, and that her gifts were being put to use in a way that was different to the way she thought it needed to look. From that day on she stopped questioning if she was in the right place or if she was doing enough. She realised she had in fact been doing her lightwork all along. She didn't need to compare herself to anyone anymore because she was exactly where she was meant to be.

No matter how many times your ego wants to convince you otherwise, everyone's gifts are equal, and all are needed. No one's purpose is any better than someone else's, they are just different expressions of lightwork. The more you believe someone else is better than you, the more you charge up their dreams instead of getting to work on your own.

Think about the next step in your dreams you are blowing up to be a big deal when really, it's not. It can just be easy and fun if you allow it to be. Now, I understand just reading that will make your ego want to shout, 'Easy for you!' Because your ego loves to create chaos out of nothing to keep you from just going for it.

Take a step back for a minute and stop focusing on all the shiny things and focus on the joy of creating and serving in the best way that you know how to. When you take the pressure off needing to be perfect, you can come back to the heart of your lightwork. The good stuff! Focus on the joy of serving and let the shiny stuff show up later when it's meant to.

Rock Your Light Reflection

WHAT ARE YOU CURRENTLY MAKING A BIGGER DEAL THAN IT NEEDS TO BE?

WHERE ARE YOU UNNECESSARILY PRESSURING YOURSELF INSTEAD OF JUST BEING IN THE JOY OF CREATING YOUR DREAMS AND LIVING YOUR LIGHTWORK?

**It's never a big deal,
unless you make it a big deal.**

YOUR LIGHTWORK IS NOT ABOUT
A LABEL, IT'S ABOUT THE
ENERGY YOU BRING.

LESSON 10

YOUR RADIANT PRESENCE IS ENOUGH

I will never forget a conversation I had with my kundalini yoga teacher, Guru Dass. There were many days whilst undergoing my yoga teacher training that I felt like a fraud and there were so many better yoga teachers than me. And there probably was. I'm not a perfect yogi. I don't meditate every day, even though I try to. I don't always drink green juice. And the more passionate I get, the more f-bombs I drop. I mean, *I can't even touch my toes,* I thought multiple times before I started teaching.

Guru Dass reminded me that you can be the perfect yogi, study all the teachings and show up to your practice every single day if you want to, but he also reiterated this: '. . . but, please, remember that you will be the most powerful teacher you can be when you just be yourself. When you bring your own energy to the teachings, people will feel it. They aren't coming for the perfect posture or to take notes on how spiritual you can speak. They are coming for your radiant presence to remind them of their own. Your purpose is to be all of you.'

From that moment on I dropped any idea of who I thought I needed to be to have an impact, and had more fun being my authentic, crazy self. Soon after, my classes started filling up. My social media engagement grew. My coaching schedule became booked out, and I felt completely in my creative power simply because I stopped trying to be like anyone else.

I knew my self-belief was going to be tested big time when I was speaking on stage with one of my best friends at one of Perth's largest wellness events. It was a big moment in my career and something I had dreamed of doing for years; I didn't want to screw it up. And as the speaking event drew closer, my fears started getting louder. *What if I say the wrong thing? What if it doesn't make sense? What if people laugh at me? Everyone else has banners. Should we print banners? I don't even have a business card, and I call myself a successful coach? What if I swear too much and people think I am unprofessional? I don't even have an elevator pitch. Does what I say even help people?*

So, I turned to my higher self for help to put an end to the story in my head that was getting me nowhere. The answer: 'People aren't wanting perfect, Trace. They just want you. Your radiant presence is enough.'

Take this reminder with you anytime you step forward to share your light with the world. Especially when your fears are having a field day and trying to knock you down from the joy of being in your lightwork. Don't worry about stumbling on your words or freaking out that you might say the wrong thing. Lay all the fancy props down and put the perfectly polished presentation on pause for a moment and remember that your radiant presence is enough. We were later notified they voted us the number one workshop of the entire event, and it wasn't because of fancy banners and business cards.

Rock Your Light Reflection

WHAT WOULD YOUR HIGHER SELF SAY TO YOU TO PUT AN END TO THE STORY THAT'S KEEPING YOU FROM SHINING YOUR RADIANT LIGHT?

You will be the most powerful teacher you can be when you just be yourself.

YOU ARE THE LIGHT

IN

*light*WORKER.

LESSON 11

EVERYONE'S LIGHT IS NEEDED, INCLUDING YOURS

If you've been on this path for a little while now, there may be a deeper calling emerging within to share more about your journey. This may come through speaking, writing, teaching, and any way you feel called to express yourself and serve others.

If you entertain the story from your ego that asks you, 'There's already enough positive people in the world—enough yoga teachers, life coaches, self-love teachers, writers—so what's the point?' Think again. I encourage you to log out of your Instagram bubble for a moment and take a walk down your local street. Look at the people rushing around stressed and anxious, or the ones who are walking around staring at the ground with a closed heart. Or look at the ones with no light in their eyes, perhaps pondering that this is just the way life is. Look at the ones staying in toxic relationships because they don't believe they are worthy of something better. Look for the ones who hate their jobs but don't believe in themselves enough to chase the beautiful dream in their heart. And look for the ones struggling to start a family and in need of support and healing. Look at the women who have forgotten their soft feminine nature is the most powerful part of them because for their whole lives they've been told that it's weak.

My partner, Luke, has been working as an engineer for eight years now, and a few years ago he craved a deeper connection to himself, and to the people around him. When we first got together, he was not interested in meditation or anything I was learning on my journey, no matter how many times I would not-so-subtly suggest it. Over the years, he witnessed me growing and changing and noticed how things showed up on my path somewhat easily. Him just witnessing me was enough to plant the seeds for when he was ready to truly receive his next steps and show up for his higher calling.

After taking a step back from engineering to explore his inner world, and in the process becoming a breathwork practitioner, he went back to engineering with a whole new energy. He soon started judging himself for feeling like if he wasn't full-time in his breathwork business or killing it as an entrepreneur, then he wasn't making an impact. I mentioned to him one day, 'But what if your greatest impact is found in merging your head and your heart gifts? What if you are needed to bring your lightwork and breathwork gifts into an industry where it is not so well spoken about? Even if all it does is offer a tool to support their anxiety and help with stress relief?' Many of us judge who is ready for our lightwork, and we close the door on opportunities to serve that are often sitting right before us.

After our conversation, Luke started teaching and offering breathwork sessions to his work colleagues on their lunchbreak hour. He realised he was getting in the way of how the Universe wanted him to use his gifts at this particular point in his journey. He had a defining moment when he underwent a 1:1 breathwork session with the CEO of the engineering company, whilst working on an oil rig in the middle of the ocean. The CEO! He stopped judging how and where his gifts were being used and got to work on just using them at any opportunity he could get.

Don't judge who is ready to learn from you or where you are being called to step up and serve. People everywhere are struggling and wanting support. They want to feel happier, less anxious, more connected. They want to feel better and you have the tools and experiences from your own journey that can help them do that. Don't let your ego get in the way. You have the teachings to offer, get out of the way and use them.

Rock Your Light Reflection

WHERE ARE YOU ALREADY USING YOUR GIFTS, OR HOW CAN YOU BRING MORE OF THEM INTO YOUR CURRENT ENVIRONMENT?

WHAT IF ALL THAT NEEDED TO CHANGE WAS A WILLINGNESS TO GET OUT OF THE WAY AND LET THE UNIVERSE SHOW YOU WHERE YOUR GIFTS ARE NEEDED?

**Your job is not to get the people;
your job is to get to work!**

DON'T DEVALUE YOUR
LIGHTWORK
JUST BECAUSE IT LOOKS
DIFFERENT TO SOMEONE
ELSE'S.

YOUR LIGHT

Our light work is needed everywhere.
In all corners, in all industries.
Stop judging where you're working it and focus on turning it up.
Down the street; behind your desk; speaking on stage or in a
1:1 intimate moment,
the only one that knows the difference
and is keeping tabs on whose purpose is better, is your ego.

There's no spiritual hierarchy, and if there is,
then your ego is the one building an empire—not you.
I know people who don't identify as a teacher and they are the
most powerful teachers I know, by how they show up to life.
Remember that your radiant presence is enough, start there.

The hairdressers are equally working their light as are the healers;
creating and caring; using their gifts to bring more beauty.
The bankers, the breathwork trainers, showing up to serve the
best way they know how.
What's more spiritual than passion and heart weaving its way
through your work.

No matter where, what, how, focus on bringing more joy and less
labels.
You may suddenly realise you've been doing your lightwork all along.
Every moment is a brand-new opportunity to either dim your light,
or bring your light.

IF YOU WANT TO
GO BIG WITH YOUR LIGHTWORK,

GO BIG

AT BEING

YOU.

PART TWO

POWER

LESSON 12

NOT EVERYTHING YOUR MIND TELLS YOU IS THE TRUTH

I want to let you in on a not-so-little secret about a particular voice in your head. One that every single person on the planet has, but not everyone is presently aware of. The first time I heard the concept of 'the voice in my head', so many things made sense to me. Often, we think we're the only one with a voice telling us that we aren't good enough, smart enough, pretty enough... the list goes on. When I became aware of this voice, I noticed all the parts of my life in which this negative voice had been running the show and keeping me far away from the person I knew I could be. The voice in your head is also referred to as your inner critic, fear, your mean girl, or your ego, it's all the same thing. It's a voice in your head on a mission to trip you up and keep you playing small. It comes up with really clever ways to distract you from your true power and potential. And as you probably already know, it can be a real party pooper, most of the time!

Your life becomes so much more magical when you pay attention and call bullshit on the voice. We must take control of our minds and make the commitment every day to switch gears from a negative autopilot, to consciously choosing better thoughts.

It's time to get real with yourself and become conscious of how many of your thoughts each day are negative, and how many are positive and supportive. Let me paint a picture for you here. Imagine each of your positive thoughts every day—such as thoughts on gratitude, being your own cheerleader, loving yourself, focusing on abundance. In short, any thoughts that help you feel good, let's pretend they are yellow tennis balls. Now think about all the fear-based thoughts you focus on every day—such as judgement, self-criticism, blame, beating yourself up, living in the past, scarcity. Any thoughts that don't make you feel good, let's imagine these are red tennis balls. Every day you are holding a tennis racquet in your mind and hitting thoughts out into the Universe, landing in either the yellow bucket or the red bucket. Because the Universe is so generous, it matches each thought you hit out and doubles it. At the end of each day, the Universe brings you both of the buckets and you get to see which bucket has the most balls in it. Is your red bucket currently heavier than your yellow one?

Most people right now are living on fear-based autopilot and hitting red balls out into the Universe without even realising. In return, the Universe hits the same colour ball back to them and they are stuck wondering why nothing in their life is ever changing. They are stuck pointing the finger trying to blame everyone else for their own lack of happiness, instead of realising that they were the one's holding the racquet all the time. The Universe was just responding to them to keep the rally going.

You can choose victory or victimhood, but you can't choose both. Reclaiming your power starts with choosing better thoughts.

And then repeating over and over again. Start by committing to reaching for better thoughts every *single* day and see how much better life becomes. To summarise this lesson in one sentence: stop entertaining crappy thoughts that aren't moving you closer to your power and your potential.

The end.

Rock Your Light Reflection

WHAT WERE MY FIRST THREE THOUGHTS WHEN I WOKE UP THIS MORNING?

WHEN I THINK ABOUT GOING AFTER MY DREAMS, WHAT THOUGHTS POP INTO MY MIND?

NOTICE IF THEY ARE THE THOUGHTS YOU WANT TO BELIEVE IN. IF NOT; CHOOSE BETTER ONES.

Check yourself before you wreck yourself.

DIRECT YOUR _THOUGHTS_

IN THE DIRECTION

OF YOUR DESTINY.

LESSON 13

SHED YOUR SANDBAGS!

When I first started making positive changes in my life, I soon recognised how many things were no longer serving me or making me feel good. In the beginning of your awakening it can feel like you question everything in your current reality. This can be very overwhelming when you realise that half of the things you used to love doing, no longer feel good to you at all! They feel heavy, like they are bogging you down and holding you back.

When I started writing this chapter, I thought about a hot air balloon. I wondered what the heck does a hot air balloon have to do with lightwork? And then I started to think about how a hot air balloon can go so high and be so light. In order for a hot air balloon to soar to its highest potential, it sheds its sandbags!

Your sandbags may show up in the form of bad health habits that are keeping you from feeling your most radiant self. Your sand-bags may be in the form of limiting beliefs that aren't supporting you into your highest vision. Self-critical thoughts that keep you down. A toxic relationship that you know isn't good for you, but you keep convincing yourself they will get better. Hanging out in environments that no longer align with the person you really want to be. Addictions that are numbing you out of your true joy. Gossiping that leaves you feeling gross, or people pleasing that is keeping you playing small. All sandbags!

I guarantee there are things currently in your life and on your plate that feel heavy and are keeping you from soaring in the way you know you are capable of. It can feel scary at first when you know there are things in your life that you need to let go of, especially when they give you a certain identity and they are all you've ever known. Sometimes, it can almost feel like unknown territory when you let go of certain parts of yourself or your life that are no longer supporting you to be the person you want to be. It can feel naked and vulnerable. But if you trust that every time you let go of something that is no longer in alignment with the person you want to be, you create space for things that are even better.

Letting go of a job that doesn't light you up creates space for a new opportunity to step into your soul work. Letting go of toxic relationships creates space for your true soul family to find you. And letting go of emotional baggage from the past creates space for peace in your heart.

Rock Your Light Reflection

CAN YOU LOVE YOURSELF ENOUGH TO LET GO OF ALL THE SANDBAGS HOLDING YOU BACK SO YOU CAN RISE AND BE THE PERSON YOU KNOW YOU ARE HERE TO BE?

WHAT SANDBAGS ARE YOU WILLING TO DROP TO RISE TO YOUR FULL POTENTIAL?

Warning:
Once you truly drop them,
you will be happier and feel lighter
than you ever have in your whole life.

TO RISE HIGHER,
YOU MUST BECOME *lighter.*

LESSON 14

FEAR STOPS WHEN YOU START

Many of us forget that fear is part of the gig in showing up to *rock your light*. It always surprises me when I mentor women and tell them about all the fears I've faced to create what I have created. They often look at me shocked, as if to say, 'You have fears too, but you're so confident... you create so much, it just looks easy and effortless for you.'

Here's something I really want you to know. You're not so special to be the only person on the planet who has to overcome big fears to live their dreams. I'm sorry, but it's true. And isn't it nice to know you aren't alone?

Absolutely everybody has a loud, fear-based voice within that can falsely accuse them of being a fraud. It's the same voice that tells you you're not good enough, not pretty enough, not smart enough, not as talented as everyone else. It's the voice that loves to tell you to sit and scroll social media when you are already in a funky mood so you can compare yourself to the so-called perfect-skinned-million-dollar-profiles. This just puts the cherry on top of your big comparison cupcake. But, as a lightworker with big dreams, you must make it your mission to master this inner voice. Know it like the back of your hand because it will potentially get even more creative as you step into your potential and power as a lightworker.

I really got the lesson that 'fear stops when you start' as I was recording some new videos for a website relaunch. My ego was having an absolute field trip that day and was possibly the loudest it has ever been, which I now know to be a really good sign that good things are on their way. It felt like I had a severe case of fear brain fog that was desperately wanting me to throw in the towel. Nevertheless, as soon as I would press record to film myself teaching, that fear would stop, and I would get in my speaking flow. I would hit stop and end the video and the mind chatter would start again.

Despite the resistance of my ego trying to convince me to pack up for the day, I would go ahead for the second video with my fear still on volume one hundred saying things like, *This doesn't even make sense! You sound like a loser! Your skin is having a major breakout. Wait until next week? OMG you should get your hair done; no one will take you seriously. What's the point anyway, no one will even watch these.* And even as this voice got louder, the same thing continued to happen, I would press play, start speaking, and the fear-based voice in my head would disappear. Fear speaks louder when you are most in alignment with your power.

Your mind only has space for one voice at a time, so make it a good one—the conscious one. I've noticed the same thing happens whenever I am about to speak in front of people, whether it's at a yoga class, a sister circle or on stage in front of hundreds of people. The same old stories come up and try to burst my excitement bubble for serving and speaking: *Everyone else is better than you, you call yourself a Yogi . . . you are so unprofessional.*

So, I show up, speak from my heart and the fears go. Every time you show up over fear, you expand what's possible for yourself.

For your entertainment here's a behind-the-brain peek of some ego thoughts that rolled through my mind whilst writing this book: *Well you swear a lot and you didn't meditate today, and you call yourself a spiritual teacher. You haven't done yoga in a week and your Instagram bio says, kundalini yogi. You don't know big words, so how the heck will you even write this book? You are having a skin breakout yet again, you definitely can't go on a book tour looking like that. You coach on self-belief, but you're struggling to believe in yourself, fraud! You're just some freckly farm chick. Who is going to want to read this? See, you can't even finish this chapter, it's not making any sense, why bother? Do you think you're freakin' Oprah?*

It breaks my heart that people give so much attention to their fears and stay stuck waiting for their fear to leave before they give themselves permission to get out there and go for it. Knowing this inner voice of fear isn't going anywhere, you can't help but laugh at the stories and the way it will try to pull out any stops it can to *stop* you being in your full potential.

Rock Your Light Reflection

WHERE ARE YOU WAITING FOR FEAR TO MAGICALLY DISAPPEAR
BEFORE YOU GO ALL IN ON YOUR DREAMS?

My advice: Bless it and then get back to work.

FEAR <u>WON'T MOVE</u>
UNTIL YOU DO.
SO, GET MOVING.

LESSON 15

DON'T BE AFRAID TO SUCK

Imagine how much lighter things would feel if we gave ourselves full permission to not have to be perfect and killing it from the get-go. We don't see the ten years of experience behind someone who can now confidently walk out on stage and speak as if it were no big deal. So we get the idea we need to walk out with that same level of confidence on our first day at the job, but that simply isn't true. I made a commitment on day one of building my business that I wouldn't be afraid to *suck at anything* before I got *good at everything*. I even wrote that mantra on a Post-it and still remind myself of it when I am trying to convince myself that I'm not ready or that I don't know what I am doing. I have now learnt that my willingness to be perfectly imperfect is one of my greatest strengths, and it can be one of yours too if you give yourself the permission to own it.

The reason I can write the way I do today is because I wasn't ever afraid to fumble my way through my words before I found my writing flow. And, I wasn't afraid to spell something wrong before hitting publish on my first blog post many years ago. I wasn't afraid to lose my train of thought mid-sentence whilst speaking on stage and trusted that the right thought would arrive when it was meant to. I wasn't afraid of not knowing the answer when someone asked me a question. I wasn't afraid to put my work out there over and over again and allow it to get better every time.

Take a lesson out of nature's book when you see a baby giraffe learning how to use its lanky new legs. It's willingness to be vulnerable and its determination to keep going whilst learning to walk is beautiful to watch. It's not worried about looking perfect on the first step, because deep down a baby giraffe knows that the fumbling will lead to finding the flow.

Give yourself time to ground into your gifts. I encourage you to check-in with where you are tripping yourself up from starting something because you are scared to be seen in the fumbling stages. Or perhaps your ego is convincing you that you don't have the expensive equipment or the shiny extravagant website, yet. Don't use excuses such as not having the right camera, or the best microphone, or the right clothes or makeup or lighting, or whatever it might be. Most of it is just an excuse and the part of you needing and expecting everything to be perfect before you start (that inner voice, remember).

I filmed my first online kundalini yoga program using an iPhone, trusting and knowing the energy I was pouring into each video was just as important as the pixels. Before I had a fancy microphone, I would use a voice recorder to record audio trainings for my clients, trusting the transmission would be clear enough until I had the resources to upgrade. In fact, I delivered my first ever online course as an in-person workshop with four women sitting on my living room floor every Sunday for six weeks. I didn't have the extra money back then to invest in hiring a yoga studio, but I knew I needed to teach. I remember thinking I didn't have pretty worksheets or even nice cushions for them to sit on. But do you think they were coming for the worksheets, or for me.

Everyone you see out there doing amazing things started exactly from where you are. All they did to get to the point where they are now was they focused on getting creative with what they *did* have, instead of getting caught up in all the things they *didn't* have. They had the willingness to be seen in their starting stages, in their draft copies.

Rock Your Light Reflection

IF I TRULY WASN'T AFRAID TO BE SEEN IN MY STARTING STAGES, WHAT WOULD I DO NOW?

> **Clip on your training wheels and get to work with what you've got.**

I AM NOT AFRAID TO SUCK
BEFORE I GET GOOD.
I AM NOT AFRAID TO SUCK
BEFORE I GET GOOD.
I AM NOT AFRAID TO SUCK
BEFORE I GET GOOD.

LESSON 16

STAY IN YOUR OWN LANE

The one thing that will turbo-boost your self-belief is to stay in your own lane. Focus on your next step. Not anyone else's. Make a commitment—right now—on your journey, to stop comparing! It's not serving you. It's the very thing that is stopping you from living your dreams and serving all the people you are here to help.

Every time you compare yourself to other people you end up going down a negative spiral about how everyone else is better than you. Or there's no point doing it because everyone else is already doing it better. This is another classic self-sabotaging move from your ego to keep you from getting out in the world and rocking your light. Stay alert to the moments when your mind will want to take you out of your flow-jo. Especially on days when you aren't feeling your best and you scroll on social media so you can see all the people online who look like millionaires. (You know what I am talking about.) This will only send you down a very unproductive path.

Be inspired by others' success, but never be distracted from your own. When you compare, you move up into your head and create a bunch of untrue stories about yourself, which instantly takes you out of your power. What I know to be true is that you can't be creating and comparing at the same time, it's impossible. When you find yourself in a negative comparing spiral, take a breath and draw your energy back down to your base and anchor it there. You need to stay grounded in who you are and what your own vision is. Otherwise you will end up sending all your creative energy in someone else's direction and not to your own dreams.

It can be really easy to see other people out there killing it at their goals when we are just starting out and thinking we need to look, speak or write just like them to be successful. I experienced this often when I first started my business and saw many other coaches doing amazing things. I idolised certain people in the coaching industry who I looked up to so much, it made me always feel small and not good enough. They were so much prettier and smarter than me. So I thought. I felt like I needed to wear clothes they would wear or speak in a way that was perfect and poetic, otherwise I would not be successful like them. Yet every single time I tried to be like somebody else, nothing in my life would flow. I would feel uninspired, not good enough and it felt like someone was choking me when all I wanted to do was speak my truth and do things my way.

The craziest thing that I realised in this whole wheel of comparison was that as I was comparing myself to another woman in her power, someone else was comparing themselves to me. And then another woman was comparing themselves to the woman that was comparing herself to me. What a waste of our precious time and energy!

I really want you to know that the world doesn't want the watered-down version of you that comes from comparing doing your soul work the same way everyone else is. It is time to really own all of who you are, especially your quirks and badass intuitive gifts, and share them unapologetically with the world.

Rock Your Light Reflection

WHO AM I CURRENTLY COMPARING MYSELF TO?

WRITE THE NAMES OF THE PEOPLE DOWN!

WHAT IS IT THEY HAVE THAT IS BEGGING TO BE ACKNOWLEDGED WITHIN ME THAT I AM NOT FULLY OWNING WITHIN MYSELF, AND HOW CAN I OWN IT TOO?

**We haven't got time to compare,
we've got magic to share!**

STOP COMPARING,

START CREATING.

LESSON 17

THE ONLY ONE JUDGING YOU IS YOU

When most people build their dreams, they become terrified of being seen in the early stages of their vision. They put so much pressure on themselves to fill up workshops, have sold out retreats, or to have a fully booked business all within a week. If they don't have a booked-out event, retreat, or schedule in that time they see themselves as a failure believing that no one will take them seriously.

I love the humility that comes from pouring your heart into your lightwork, especially in the early days. I love witnessing people courageously putting their work out into the world, hoping it will inspire someone else to step up and do the same. When you put your energy into worrying what other people will think of you, you are not taking the courageous action that is necessary to bring your lightwork into the world. I want to remind you that other people will take you seriously when you take yourself seriously. Be proud of who you are and the message you want to share with the world.

When I first started sharing my work online, sometimes it felt like the only person liking my work was my mum. Even though I could see on the back end of my website that hundreds of people were reading and viewing my work, it felt like the comment section was covered in cobwebs and crickets. I knew they could feel it, even if they didn't say they did. My lack of likes didn't make me stop, because I knew I had work to do and the lack of likes wasn't going to keep this lightworker from rocking her light!

You might feel it's time to put your soul work out into the world, or to write about things you are passionate about, or to teach workshops on topics that really light you up. Once again, don't become stuck in a loop of worrying about how other people might judge you, or about how many people will show up in the beginning. The only one that knows the difference between two and two hundred, is your ego.

> Press publish.
> Share the post.
> Teach the workshop.
> Start the business.
> Enrol in the course.
> Quit the job.
> Change direction, again.
> Start fresh.
> Say, no.
> Say, yes.
> Speak up.
>
> Let yourself be seen.
>
> Own your light.
> No one cares that it isn't perfect, but you.

Rock Your Light Reflection

IF YOU CONSTANTLY COMPLAIN NOT ENOUGH PEOPLE ARE SHOWING UP AND LIKING YOUR STUFF, TAKE A CHECK-IN AND ASK YOURSELF THESE QUESTIONS.

HOW AM I SHOWING UP? AM I HERE FOR THE PRAISE AND THE STAGE? AM I HERE FOR HOW MANY LIKES I WILL BE VALIDATED BY ON SOCIAL MEDIA? WHAT WOULD CHANGE IF I STOPPED CARING ABOUT THE NUMBERS AND FOCUSED MORE ON HAVING FUN AT BEING WHO I CAME HERE TO BE?

**Your ego will regularly try to stop you from sharing your work.
Show up and share anyway.**

BELIEVE IN <u>YOURSELF</u>
THE WAY YOU BELIEVE
IN YOUR BEST FRIEND.

LESSON 18

GET LIT ON THE LEVEL YOU'RE AT

Do you ever tell yourself that you should be further ahead than where you are now, or that everyone else is so much better than you? Perhaps that you should have all your shit together by now and be making your millions? Maybe you've been in business for a few years and you're beating yourself up that your following isn't big enough or you're not fully booked like you thought you would be. I want you to know that you are exactly at the level you're supposed to be now. You aren't gifted the next level until you've mastered the level you're at. And that is a good thing! If something hasn't happened by now, it doesn't mean it never will. It just means it wasn't meant to have happened yet.

You can't demand that you deserve $2,000 without respecting, appreciating or knowing what to do with the $200 that you've already received. And if you're not fully showing up for the three clients you already have, why would you think you'd be ready for the ten that you don't have and are complaining about? I see people all the time complaining that they aren't getting enough social media interaction, or they don't have enough people coming to their events. Which I understand can be very frustrating when you are pouring your whole heart into your work. But have you ever thought maybe you're not being gifted more because you aren't truly appreciating what's already here?

If you don't show up to actively and creatively participate in the level you are at, why would the Universe gift you more?

Rock Your Light Reflection

BE HONEST AND ASK YOURSELF THIS: IF YOU RECEIVED EVERY SINGLE THING YOU WANTED TOMORROW — THE THOUSANDS OF FOLLOWERS, THE BOOK DEAL, THE FIFTY NEW CLIENTS, THE SIX-FIGURE INCOME— WOULD YOU ACTUALLY BE ABLE TO HANDLE AND HOLD IT? WOULD YOU KNOW WHAT TO DO WITH IT? MAYBE, BUT PROBABLY NOT. EVERYTHING IS MOVING INTO YOUR FIELD AT THE PERFECT SPEED TO MATCH WHERE YOU'RE AT. THIS IS WHY DOING THE DRAFT COPY OF WHAT YOU WANT TO CREATE BEFORE IT IS CREATED IS SO IMPORTANT AS IT TRAINS YOUR BODY TO RECEIVE AND HOLD IT.

You are receiving everything you can energetically handle.

YOUR VISION ISN'T IN A RUSH,
SO WHY ARE YOU?

LESSON 19

SELF-TRUST IS YOUR SUPERPOWER

If you are reading this book, chances are you've been guided to it at exactly the right time to help give you the courage to take the next steps and go all in on your dreams. I bet your intuition has been not-so-subtly nudging you in a new direction and giving you the green light to bring your dreams to life.

Maybe right now you're stuck pretending you don't know the answer, or you don't know what you truly want to be doing when in fact the opposite is true. You might feel called to leave a job that isn't lighting you up anymore. But you don't want to let your boss down who has invested so much time in training you up for a role by changing careers. You don't want to let your parents down when you ditch the uni degree to chase the real dream in your heart and not the dream they want for you. You don't want to let a business partner down by changing direction and admitting your heart just isn't in it anymore and your gifts want to be expressed in a whole new way.

When you have truly committed to living the highest vision for your life, it will require a level of trust in yourself that you didn't even think was possible. There will be crucial moments on your path that will require you to show up, lean in and trust yourself when it makes absolutely no sense to do so. We are living in times where listing out all the 'on paper' logical reasons aren't necessarily the way we make decisions. They are outdated ways of living, and you are here to help birth a new way of living and leading from the heart.

You can't just preach about choosing love over fear, you've got to live it. You'll have to say 'yes' to opportunities you don't truly feel ready for. You'll have to share your words before you've fully grounded into your voice. You'll have to show up to a vision you can't fully understand yet, but you just feel it so deeply.

The thing that trips us up is that this superpower is invisible. You can't always see what's trying to come into your life, be it a new job, a new relationship, a completely different stream of abundance, a huge opportunity, but you can *feel it*. I encourage you to lean more into trusting this feeling because that gut feeling you have is the most accurate GPS system you will ever come across. It's set at exactly the right direction your soul is meant to be heading. Remember, the Universe will keep guiding you the more you lean into the guidance.

If you are experiencing a mix of feeling extremely nervous and ridiculously excited, then you're right on track, my friend. When you truly step into your power as a lightworker, the Universe will continually bring in opportunities for you to share your light and your gifts. You're the only one that's stopping it because you're getting all up in your head and making it about you. Look for an opportunity to teach a meditation group. Offer a pro bono coaching session to a mum who needs extra support. Lend a book to a friend who is going through a rough patch. Offer support to a stranger who is asking for help.

The Universe is always bringing you opportunities that are an exact match to where you're at and what it knows you can handle. So, know these opportunities wouldn't be falling into your lap if they weren't meant for you. It's not about being perfect. It's about trusting yourself and showing up for your dreams exactly as you are.

Rock Your Light Reflection

YOUR INTUITION IS CURRENTLY LEADING YOU TOWARDS WHAT YOU HAVE BEEN OVERTHINKING FOR MONTHS NOW, SO ASK YOURSELF: IF I REALLY AND TRULY TRUST MYSELF, WHAT WOULD I DO?

Confidence is sexy, but self-trust is sexier.

FLEX YOUR *self-trust*
AS MUCH AS YOU FLEX YOUR
BICEPS.

LESSON 20

THE UNIVERSE HAS THE HOOK-UPS

I've lost count of the amount of times the Universe has had my back. It's led me to the right people and experiences at exactly the right time—helping me spread my message and get my lightwork out into the world.

The day my book proposal was rejected was a turning point for me. I had been pouring my heart into the proposal, showing up, reaching out to people for help and working my manifesting magic as best I could. I'd been journaling about how it felt to see my book on airport shelves and my friends sending me photos of it in their local bookshops. I was all in. Yet it didn't go to plan. It didn't go to *my* plan. Of course, I was upset at first. I could have thrown in the towel and thought maybe my book wasn't as good as I believed it to be, or that I wasn't meant to be an author. Within two minutes of the inner stories rising, I chose a better story to believe. I knew the power of this book because I felt it. I knew there was a creative solution to what was appearing to be a stop sign. Trust me when I tell you that when a roadblock appears, your angels are already onto it.

As soon as I found out I was *rejected* I went to my meditation cushion and sat still, tuning in to my inner guidance. I asked the Universe to show me the next step or to give me a clear sign of what I needed to know, with full willingness to take action on exactly what it would tell me. I asked, 'Show me what to do next and I will show up.' I received a clear message almost instantly, 'Stay open. You weren't meant to publish with someone who would try to change the way you use your voice, that's a gift of yours that can't be edited. You are to write this book in the way it wants to be written. There's a better plan coming.' I felt a jolt of energy, and I knew that was enough of a sign to trust that the next step wasn't far away. I just needed to pay attention. I know whenever I feel the energy in my body, the Universe is already getting to work.

And the Universe delivered. At the time, I was working with a web designer who has become a close friend. I'd told her about the book. She asked me if I'd heard back and if I'd received the book deal, to which my answer was no. She then replied, 'I think you should meet Natasha; she is a client of mine. She's an editor and is just about to open her publishing house. I have a feeling you two are meant to connect.' I'd never heard of Natasha until that moment, because I wasn't meant to until then. Submitting the proposal gave me the deadline to start my draft copy, so I had my book proposal on file and ready to go. I didn't think twice. I knew this was the Universe hooking me up. Within ten minutes I emailed Natasha explaining the connection and asked if she could help. To which her reply was: 'I'm not currently offering writing mentoring. Although, I'm getting a nudge from the Universe that I am the one to help you bring your book to life, so let's do it.' It turns out the Universe had a better plan than what I could see, and that rejection led to an even better connection.

Do you really think the Universe would have gifted you a vision without having a plan of everything you need? When you show up and commit to doing whatever you can on your side of the show, you magnetise the next step to you. However, you can't open the second door without stepping through the first one. The money you invest in your business, the people who help you bring it to life, the connections or the opportunities to spread your message will show up for you when you show up for you. Never forget that higher guidance is always available to you when you tune in to listen. The signs are always there waiting for you, so stop ruling them out as a coincidence and pay attention to them. If you want to keep moving forward on your mission, then don't just ask, act!

Rock Your Light Reflection

TAKE A MOMENT, CLOSE YOUR EYES AND FEEL THE SUPPORT OF THE UNIVERSE,

SAY THIS PRAYER,

I OPEN MY MIND, HANDS AND HEART TO RECEIVING ALL THE CREATIVE POSSIBILITIES AND RESOURCES THAT I NEED TO SERVE AT MY FULL CAPACITY AND KEEP MOVING FORWARD WITH MY LIGHTWORK. I AM LISTENING TO THE UNIVERSE'S GUIDANCE AND I AM READY TO TAKE ACTION ON WHAT I HEAR.

Don't just ask, act!

REJECTION

IS JUST A

REDIRECTION.

LESSON 21

FEAR OF SUCCESS IS KEEPING YOU SMALL

If you're like most people, one of the biggest blocks keeping you from sharing your light with the world right now is the fear of failure. It scares you to invest in yourself because it might not work, or that you will make the wrong decision and regret it. This knee jerk response is an excuse that stops most people from going all in on their dreams because of the fear of failure. We tell ourselves there's no point going for something because we probably won't be able to achieve it.

I want to help change your perception of failure, so there isn't so much energetic charge and fear around it. The truth is, you don't ever actually fail at anything. You just collect data about what works and what doesn't. It's as simple as that. Building your dreams is simply a collection of mini experiments, which your mind could be mistakenly labelling under 'failures', in which you keep refining and practicing with until you nail the perfect ingredients. Creation is an ongoing expansion that has no end point, it just keeps widening. Really let that sink in.

Now that we have cleared that up a bit, let's get to the real issue here, your fear of success. I don't believe your biggest block right now is your fear of failure. I believe it's your fear of your dreams coming true and what that might mean if you get what you really want. Most of us are so scared to be our most healthy, happy, abundant, successful selves because when we are growing up we are taught to be quiet. We're told to not make a scene, not to be an attention seeker, and not to own our strengths just in case we make someone else feel bad about theirs. In other words, we have been taught from the get-go to dim our light to keep other people comfortable.

This might have worked in the past, but it doesn't take a rocket scientist to know that this is absolutely not the time to be dimming our light any longer. If the world is going to keep shifting towards higher consciousness where more people live from their heart space, this is the time for lightworkers to be loud and proud. To courageously own their light and to shine it brighter than ever. You don't outshine others; you shine *for* others.

At first it can feel really scary to own your light, and it will probably rock the boat a bit with the people around you. That's because it would be so much easier to keep hiding and dimming your light, which is why most people do it. They stay playing small and waste their energy judging and getting jealous of other people who are going for it. It's really easy to stay in your comfort zone and never take the leap towards your dreams. It's easy to ignore your intuition when it's trying to lead you in an even better direction. And at the end of the day, you don't even have to answer the call of your soul if you don't want to. But I'll let you in on a little secret, life will become *very* painful if you don't.

To keep you in your comfort zone and away from your highest potential, your mind will unconsciously create stories of what might happen if your dreams actually work. It starts future projecting to create resistance from you rolling your sleeves up and getting down and dirty with your dreams. This is a really sneaky and subtle form of self-sabotage that is hard to catch out until you do some deeper digging.

✦ Rock Your Light Reflection

TAKE SOME REFLECTION TIME HERE TO REALLY LOOK AT WHAT IS CURRENTLY HOLDING YOU BACK FROM ALLOWING YOURSELF TO SHINE BRIGHTER AND TO REALLY GO FOR IT WITH YOUR GOALS.

ASK YOURSELF, WHAT AM I SCARED MIGHT HAPPEN IF I ACTUALLY PULL THIS THING OFF? WHO AM I AFRAID I MIGHT OUTSHINE?

✦

LET ME LEAD WITH SOME EXAMPLES HERE THAT MIGHT HELP THIS PROCESS:

I'M SCARED THAT IF I BECOME SUCCESSFUL, MAYBE MY FRIENDS WILL START TO NOT LIKE ME ANYMORE AND THINK, 'WHO DOES SHE THINK SHE IS?'

I'M SCARED THAT IF MY BUSINESS GOES TO THE NEXT LEVEL, I WILL HAVE TO WORK HARDER AND WILL HAVE LESS TIME WITH MY FAMILY AND THEY WILL RESENT ME.

I'M SCARED THAT IF I CREATE MORE ABUNDANCE, I WILL HAVE TO PAY OFF MY DEBTS AND NOT RELY ON OTHERS FOR HANDOUTS ANYMORE.

I'M SCARED THAT IF I GET HEALTHY AND START TAKING BETTER CARE OF MYSELF, I WILL HAVE NOTHING IN COMMON WITH MY FRIENDS WHO ONLY WANT TO PARTY ALL THE TIME.

I'M SCARED THAT IF I KEEP GROWING AND DO ALL OF THIS INNER WORK THAT IS REALLY LIGHTING ME UP, I'LL REALISE I NEED TO LEAVE MY PARTNER.

I'M SCARED THAT IF I ENROL IN THE COURSE AND COMPLETE IT, I'LL ACTUALLY HAVE TO SHOW UP FOR MY LIGHTWORK AND STOP HIDING MY TRUE SELF WITH THE WORLD.

Keep digging deep for the gold,
because it will be a game changer
when you realise that *nothing*
has to change unless you choose it to.

YOU NEVER FAIL,
YOU JUST REDIRECT YOUR
ENERGY.

LESSON 22

YOU CAN HANDLE IT

When I took a big leap in my business that had been in the works for many years, I was being seen and received at a new level and I could feel it. I'd hit a point where life was really flowing. My business was booming, my relationships were overflowing with joy, and my creativity was in the best flow I'd ever felt. I was showing up, and it felt amazing to be in my power and truly own who I was here to be. I was so proud of myself. Everything was falling into place and only getting better and better. And then, because it felt so good, I subconsciously got scared that I would stuff it up.

One day during this particular time of expansion, I woke up with an anxious feeling in my stomach. Usually in these times I can reach into my toolkit and get to the bottom of it pretty quickly. On this day I couldn't shake it. I tried to journal about it, meditate on it, talk it out with my friends. Nothing would shift. I couldn't figure out exactly what was making me feel this way as everything was going so well on the outside.

I hit the gym with a good friend who was also my personal trainer.

He'd been witnessing me going through this growth and was cheering me on the whole way, but he could feel something was up for me that day. I began my regular workout and headed to the squat rack. The Universe often speaks to you through people, so you get the message loud and clear. I felt the anxiousness bubbling up in my stomach. As I lifted the weights, I said to him, 'I can't do it, it's too much.' There was no pause between my words and his response, 'Trace, you've done the work, you're strong and you can handle all of it.' As soon as I heard the words, I burst out crying in the middle of the gym. I knew he was referring to being able to handle the amount of weight resting across my shoulders. But the Universe was referring to trusting myself in handling the next level of power and success I was experiencing.

> I was scared to feel powerful.
> I was scared to be seen in my success.
> I was scared to feel more radiant than I'd ever felt.
> I was scared of my own light.

You may experience something similar in your life when you feel yourself feeling too healthy, light, radiant, successful, abundant, peaceful or powerful. It can feel like a part of you is trying to trip you up and convince you it won't last long or you'll probably mess it up. You won't.

These moments are usually right before you are about to shift into a new level of expansion. Things can feel a little wobbly and you might second-guess yourself. The self-doubt creeps into your mind and gets louder with a list of reasons why you should just go back into your spiritual closet where it's warm and safe. Some people refer to this stage as the contraction before the expansion. I like to think of it as the turbulence right before the take-off. Many of us when we experience moments of friction or fear bubbling up right before we are about to step into our power, get confused. We think feeling unsure must mean we are doing something wrong or maybe it isn't the right path for us. Please know these feelings are just the initiation into the next level. This is the Universe doing one last check to see if you are really committed to what you say you want.

♦ Rock Your Light Affirmation

IT IS SAFE FOR ME TO BE SEEN IN MY POWER.

The joy is in the turbulence right before the take-off. The Universe is just doing the final flight checks for you.

WHEN YOU WANT TO
TAP OUT, TAP IN.

TRUST YOUR VOICE.
TRUST YOUR HEART.
TRUST YOUR LIGHT.
YOU CAN HANDLE IT.

LESSON 23

COMMIT TO YOUR LIGHT

When you step out of the spiritual closet and own your light, you might hear crickets. Your ego is going to tell you things that aren't the truth and aren't your reality.

Every time you show up, even when you feel you are drowning in self-doubt,
> **the Universe is paying attention to your commitment to your light.**

Every time you speak your truth, even with sweaty palms and a shaky voice,
> **the Universe is paying attention to your commitment to your light.**

Every time you show up with a full heart,
> **the Universe is paying attention to your commitment to your light.**

Every time you trust that faint voice, your inner guidance, against any logical or rational thought, and you trust it anyway because you feel it so deeply,

>**the Universe is paying attention to your commitment to your light.**

Every time it terrifies you to take the next step on your path and have no idea how things will work out, but you take the step anyway,

>**the Universe is paying attention to your commitment to your light.**

Growth has taken you to this very point in your life. Every decision you've made, landed you here to read this book. You've overcome fears, doubts and you've shown up to attract the opportunities you now find yourself in. You were scared, and you showed up anyway. Don't forget how far you've come by focusing on how far you have to go.

✦ LIGHTWORKER
PERMISSION SLIP

I,_____,on this day, _____,sign this potent permission slip and commit to believing in myself, no matter what, and showing up fully for the great work I am here to do and bring to the world.

_____
Signature

Hand on heart, I solemnly declare and commit to being a Lightworker.

PART THREE

PROSPERITY

LESSON 24

YOU ARE A NATURAL RECEIVER

If we want to be abundant, we have to be cool with the fact that receiving is part of the abundance magic, just as giving is. I hear stories all the time that keep women from thriving with their finances. 'I am great at giving, I just feel bad about receiving.' 'I'm not good at it and it makes me feel weird.'

The truth is, you are receiving all day, every day, without even realising you are. The first thing you did in this lifetime as a newborn was to receive that first breath you took. By receiving that breath; it gave you life. When you allow yourself to receive in the way that life truly wants to give to you, you feel supported, nourished and well. When you are depriving yourself from the natural flow of the Universe, there is an imbalance.

Think about how much joy you experience when you give someone that you love a gift from your heart. Perhaps it's something you made for them you just know they will love, and it lights you up so much thinking about the look on their face when they receive your unexpected surprise. The Universe can feel it when you tell yourself you aren't worthy of all the beauty, love, joy, abundance and success that it wants to shower you with, just for being you. It's like a kid deciding to return a present to Santa Claus because they feel they don't deserve it. Can you imagine? You are doing this all the time when you rob the Universe, or even other people, of being in the joy of giving you a beautiful gift. Let's call this gift 'your dreams all wrapped up'. And the Universe is bringing you all these resources to support you on your mission, but then you have a crappy story about how you are bad at receiving. It's like the mailman delivering you a parcel and you not opening the door. And here you are trying your hardest to manifest your dreams, whilst simultaneously keeping the door shut and projecting outwards: return to sender.

I encourage you to take on a new story. The new story of *I am a natural receiver.* Try it on for size and see how it fits. Notice everything you are receiving on a daily basis, and not just in the form of money. The compliment from your partner, a text from your best friend, a smile at a stranger, the nutritious meal you just ate, the warm rays from the sun, a full breath of air on your next inhale. You are even receiving the words and energy of this book as you are reading.

Receiving is easy and natural and fun. It is an essential part of life and allowing yourself to receive money for the amazing work you put out to help the world is exactly what the Universe intended.

If you are going to have an impact in the world in the way that you truly know you are capable of, then you have to let the Universe support you to get there. If you don't let the Universe support your lightwork, then you will become unbalanced, resentful and burnt out because the giving side of the scale is stacked much higher than the receiving.

Rock Your Light Reflection

DO YOU CLOSE DOWN AND FEEL AWKWARD WHEN ASKING
FOR MONEY?

DO YOU QUESTION YOUR COACHING OR CREATING FEES?

DO YOU FEEL NOURISHED AND ENERGISED FROM SERVING, OR DO
YOU FEEL DRAINED AND DEPLETED WHEN YOU FINISH?
(THIS CAN BE AN IMBALANCE IN EXCHANGE.)

DO YOU PROCRASTINATE IN FOLLOWING UP WITH INVOICES WHEN
YOU NEED TO?

DO YOU PRETEND YOU DON'T CARE ABOUT MAKING MONEY INSTEAD
OF ALLOWING YOURSELF TO BE COMPLETELY SUPPORTED AND
NOURISHED BY YOUR LIGHTWORK?

I am a natural receiver.

WHEN I RECEIVE,
EVERYONE RECEIVES.

LESSON 25

INSTALL A NEW MONEY MINDSET

Many people would rather just dust their negative money beliefs and habits under the rug or put them in the too-hard basket than get to work on choosing a better money mindset. Before you install a new money mindset, you need to clean out some of the old software and autopilot programming in your mind. This is keeping you from having a high-vibrational relationship with money in the way that you want to.

So, let's start at the beginning and unravel some of your first money experiences that have shaped the way you see money. This goes back to when you were younger and were a sponge-absorbing-everything in your environment, including the way people in your life were acting and communicating about money as you were growing up. If that wasn't a positive experience, you must remember they were only doing the best they could with what they had, so let's look back through the lens of compassion only. We need to look back and track, not just how people around us were talking about money, but the energy they were giving off whenever money was the topic of conversation. Were your parents hushing you into another room to play with your toys whenever they spoke about budgeting or money? Were they turning their nose up and gossiping about other people with a lot of wealth which lead you to believe that people will judge and talk about you if you have too much money? Or were they arguing constantly about money, meaning you believed money causes arguments?

A new level of *abundance* requires a new level of thinking.

Another important part of how you relate to money is to think back to the first time you ever thought about someone in your life as having power and abundance. Knowing the first person who pops into your mind when you think about power, usually linked to money, is crucial. It could be someone you've seen on television, or it could be someone in your life that you know. Identify who this person is for you. Is this an example of someone living with their abundance in a way that makes you want to align with? It's time to align with a new version of power and abundance that stems from the heart, not an outdated model that is laced with greed, control or competition. If you are associating money with people in the world that don't align with you, such as certain presidents whose values don't match your own or celebrities that have a lot of money—and the drama to match it—that's not going to make you want to cosy up with more abundance anytime soon. In fact, you will repel it.

Instead, focus your attention on an example of someone who is pairing money with heart and service and using what they have to create better in the world. That is a lightworker showing you what you can do with *abundance*.

✦ *Rock Your Light Reflection*

WHO HAS AN ABUNDANT BANK ACCOUNT AND AN ABUNDANT HEART
TO MATCH IT YOU CAN ALIGN WITH FROM NOW ON?

**Abundance is just an amplifier.
Your generous heart will only become more
generous with money on your side.**

BELIEVE IN ABUNDANCE
every day,
NOT JUST PAYDAY.

LESSON 26

ABUNDANCE COMES IN MANY FORMS

Whenever people hear the word abundance, the first thing they usually think about and look for is money. It can feel like a bit of a smack in the face when you are saying all your money affirmations, pulling the abundance angel card four days in a row, and still nothing seems to shift or accumulate in your bank account. The one thing we misinterpret is that abundance isn't just money. Abundance comes in many forms and in many differently wrapped packages. If money is the only form of abundance you're looking for, you won't be accessing the abundance that's available to you in the present moment.

Shift your focus onto what is flowing and going well in your life—right now—and keep the energy of abundance moving through you and project it out into the world. Although your bank account isn't reflecting the number that you think you *need* right now, take a pause from constantly checking the balance and focus your energy on everything that *has* flowed into your life over the last few months. Maybe you've been meeting new and like-minded people, or your relationships have thrived, or you feel more joyful and connected than ever before. Maybe you are on a health kick and feel the best you have ever felt in your body, or your spiritual practice is really rocking your world right now and you feel more in tune than ever. You might attract job opportunities, or a friend might offer to help babysit so you can have a few extra hours to work on your business or take some well-deserved time out for yourself. You might feel an *abundance* of new and creative ideas, energy and excitement for your life. These are all reminders that abundance is already showing up, just in a different form. The ego always looks for money. Truth is, there is more to abundance than money.

So, ramp up that abundant feeling by focusing on what is flowing in your life, knowing that this feel-good-energy will filter into your financial channels soon. When you feel more excited and inspired by your life, your energy levels go up, and when you focus on feeling good, new opportunities, ideas and creative possibilities arrive.

Lack is just an illusion that is amplified when you start to future trip. This only scatters your energy and fuels the fear about needing to know exactly how the money will show up and when. Bring your energy back into the present moment and crank up the appreciation for what you have and what abundance is already here for you.

Instead of feeding the 'I never have enough' fear-based programming in your mind, break the cycle and feed thoughts of 'I have everything I need in this present moment, and it's more than enough.'

You have more than enough air to breathe. More than enough energy to wake up in the morning. More than enough water to drink, food to eat. And you definitely have more than enough love to give.

Rock Your Light Reflection

WHAT IS CURRENTLY FLOWING IN YOUR LIFE?

WHAT DO YOU CURRENTLY HAVE MORE THAN ENOUGH OF?

WHERE HAS ABUNDANCE SHOWED UP IN YOUR LIFE THIS YEAR THAT YOU DIDN'T NOTICE BECAUSE IT WASN'T JUST MONEY?

> **I have everything I need in this present moment, and it's more than enough.**

I HAVE <u>EVERYTHING I NEED</u>
IN THIS PRESENT MOMENT TO
TAKE MY NEXT STEP.

LESSON 27

COMMIT TO A HIGH-VIBRATIONAL RELATIONSHIP WITH MONEY

A few years ago, I knew that my money beliefs needed some serious work. It was time to get real. I knew if I was going to really live to my full potential and serve in the way that I wanted, then money would be a part of that gig. The more I allowed myself to love money, the more it appeared to love me back. I knew I needed to earn more to continually invest back into my vision. I knew that investing in my lightwork would be a great investment for the whole collective. It was a win-win. I was the only one getting in the way.

I scribbled these words down on a Post-it note: I commit to a high-vibrational relationship with money. And I stuck it on my bathroom mirror so it would constantly remind me of my commitment. I was ready and willing to show up, for real this time. I made a pact with myself that I was only thinking good thoughts about money from now on. I wouldn't chuck a tantrum every time a bill came in. I wouldn't get mad at the Universe for not bringing me more cash when I wasn't truly acknowledging the ways it was already supporting me. And I sure as heck wouldn't keep waiting for someone else to solve my money problems for me. If I was going to be an example of how anyone could follow their heart and be abundant from living their lightwork, then I knew I'd have to clean a few things up first.

There are never tests. They are opportunities for embodiment. I often laugh at how quickly the Universe gets moving once you have truly committed to showing up and doing the money work. The day after I stuck the Post-it note on the mirror, I received my first ever fine from the police. They caught me with my phone in my hand at the traffic lights. I knew this was my first opportunity to embody my new money mentality. The Tracey yesterday would have chucked a tantrum seeing the $450 on-the-spot fine. The Tracey today was committed to a high-vibrational relationship with money. I received the fine with the biggest grin on my face that must have confused the officer. For once in my life, I was happy and grateful to receive this fine. I paid it the second I got home, without crying about it, without charging it up to be a bigger deal than it needed to be. I just let it be easy. And I learnt my lesson to be responsible for my actions as a lightworker too. No more phone—check. The thing is, it's never about the amount and everything to do with how you feel about the amount. I got the memo loud and clear, and my bank account has only soared since that day.

Another time I was walking along the South Perth foreshore in what was about to be exercise-peak hour with my friend, Zsuzsa. We talked about how excited we were to be working on our abundance mindsets and attracting new opportunities into our lives. We felt all the high vibes and were so grateful for all the ways money was flowing in our lives. There were so many people walking and riding along the footpath as we preached out our money mantras in conversation. Then, as I looked down, a $50 note was sitting at my feet in the middle of this busy footpath. We looked at each other and shrieked in disbelief, looking around to see if someone was looking for it. We realised this was the Universe directly responding to the fun we were having creating new money beliefs and stories. The Universe was giving us evidence of the abundance coming in creative, unexpected ways. Our job in that moment was not to feel unworthy and feel bad about it. It was to joyfully and gratefully receive it, physically, with both hands and to openly keep the river of abundance flowing.

Rock Your Light Reflection

IF YOU WERE TO DRAW A LINE IN THE SAND FROM THIS
MOMENT ON AND COMMIT TO A HIGH-VIBRATIONAL RELATIONSHIP
WITH MONEY, WHAT WOULD NEED CLEANING UP? START NOW WITH
NOTICING THE THOUGHTS AND BELIEFS YOU HAVE ABOUT MONEY,
CHOOSING MORE EMPOWERED ONES WHERE NEEDED, AND NOTICE
THE RIPPLES THAT FLOW FROM THAT ALONE.

> **I allow myself to love money,**
> **and for money to love me back.**

I COMMIT TO A
HIGH-VIBRATIONAL
RELATIONSHIP WITH MONEY,
NO MATTER WHAT.

LESSON 28

ABUNDANCE FOLLOWS JOY

It is my greatest wish that more people put the pros and cons list down and follow a path that brings them the most joy. I deeply believe that *abundance* follows *joy*. When you commit to the vision in your heart, the abundance you feel on the inside will always be reflected on the outside. No matter how long it might take you and how creative you need to get along the way. There have been so many times I have trusted in this lesson and know that abundance shows up if I stay committed to my heart's path. I have taken many risks based on choosing to lean in to the direction that brings me the most joy, not based on the path that was the one I *should* have been taking. We're often told when we are growing up to 'do the right thing', 'living your dreams is only for lucky people,' or 'don't be stupid, you need to get a safe and respectable job', and it makes us believe our gifts aren't enough unless they meet certain on-paper-expectations. The thing that cracks me up is that most people who are living with a 'safe job' are the ones who are highly anxious, stressed, disconnected and creatively dry. It might be safe, but is it satisfying to your soul?

One of the greatest ways to unlock your abundance is to go where your energy most *wants* to go. Follow the path that is pulling you towards joy and excitement, even when you don't know exactly what it will look like or how it will turn out. You will feel it. Maybe right now you want to move into a new home and trying to decide between two open inspections. I invite you to let your logical mind take a back seat and ask yourself, which home brings us more joy? Of course, we don't want to be reckless with our decisions. But how many times are we turning down beautiful experiences and opportunities for joy based on what we think we should do versus what we really and truly want to do. What if your dreams are only one joyful decision away from your current reality? I'm certain the absolute worst thing you think could happen is nowhere near as painful as staying where you don't want to be.

When I first graduated as a life coach, I felt the brightest when I spoke to and taught groups of women. There was something magical in the energy of group work that made my whole-body light up with excitement and ideas. At the time, many people around me suggested I take on face-to-face clients, as though it were the unwritten law that all coaches needed to follow to be successful. I was trying so hard to follow this rule. Until one day I just followed the joy in my heart to start speaking, teaching and mentoring groups of women. As soon as I trusted this feeling and followed the joy, my business started booming.

Say yes to the things that are most calling from your heart. Joy is a magnet for abundance, creativity and opportunities to support your purpose. Joy is always giving you clues in the right direction; you've just got to be brave enough to follow them.

Rock Your Light Reflection

IF YOU ARE CURRENTLY TRYING TO MAKE A DECISION IN YOUR LIFE
AND YOU ARE UP IN YOUR HEAD ABOUT THE LOGISTICS, LIKE
ENROLLING TO DO YOGA TRAINING, REGISTERING TO START A
BUSINESS, MOVING TO A NEW CITY, CHOOSING A DANCE CLASS
OVER THE GYM, ASK YOURSELF: WHAT WILL BRING ME THE MOST
JOY? AND THEN DO IT!

**Your vision wants to support you
just as much as you want to support it.**

JOY IS THE ARROW,

ABUNDANCE
IS THE BULLSEYE.

LESSON 29

JEALOUSY IS JUST LACK

Do you ever get jealous of other people? I'm sure the answer will be yes. Jealousy shows up in many ways and is a low vibe pulling you back into scarcity.

Jealousy creates a story that you lack something, or that other people have more than you. It wants to make you feel smaller. This only fuels the 'I don't have enough' story in your mind and solidifies this belief in your reality. You can catch jealousy and release it every time it shows up. It's not always easy, but it's always possible.

The fastest way to be more successful is to celebrate other people and their success as if it were your own. Train your mind to do this instead of going into the ego's default setting of jealousy or comparison. You become more attractive to abundance when you have no resistance to appreciating the abundance in others. Notice the resistance to success that is showing up in your life right now in the form of jealousy because all this will do is keep it further away from you.

Being jealous is a tendency that we need to grow out of if we want to create the abundance that's available to us in our lives. Instead of sitting around and pointing the finger thinking 'it's easy for them', why don't we get excited for what they have created? We can do this with the deep knowing that they are only a lighthouse showing us what is also possible for us to create too. We have to clean up this autopilot response, otherwise we will always have this belief that we are 'getting left behind' or that somebody else has more than us. Therefore we have less and confirm the story from our fears that we never have enough. Heads up: if you are reading this book, guess what, you have more than enough, you're just living in an outdated thought pattern that is keeping you feeling anything but abundant. Believe in abundance before the abundance shows up and it will stay with you. That's because you have trained your body and your mind to believe in it so deeply that the Universe will catch up with your beliefs and call it in.

I really want to encourage you to get real with yourself here about the ways you are letting jealousy keep you far away from the abundance you deserve. Are you waiting for someone else to come and save you from your money stuff rather than choosing to get excited about creating abundance and success for yourself? It's up to us lightworkers to commit to dissolving every single fear-based story that we have floating around our minds and constantly reach for new ones. You are powerful, and you have the potential to change your current situation.

✦ Rock Your Light Reflection

MAKE AN HONEST LIST OF THE PEOPLE YOU ARE JEALOUS OF.

THEN PINPOINT EXACTLY WHAT IT IS ABOUT THEM THAT MAKES YOU JEALOUS AND WRITE THEM DOWN. DO YOU SEE ANY PATTERNS DEVELOPING IN YOUR BELIEFS?

DO YOU SEE WHERE YOUR JEALOUSY CAN BE AN ARROW POINTING YOU TOWARD WHERE YOU ARE HIDING FROM YOUR OWN POWER?

Commit to show up when things come up, especially the not-so-pretty parts like jealousy.

YOU ARE ONLY JEALOUS OF

someone

WHEN YOU'VE FORGOTTEN

you

ARE THAT POWERFUL TOO.

LESSON 30

UPGRADE YOUR UNDIES

Have you taken a good look at your underwear drawer lately? If you are upgrading your money mindset, start with upgrading your underwear. Why? I hear you ask. Part of this is because walking around with holes and over-stretched underwear won't ever make you feel abundant, but the real lesson is that everything holds an energy, including your undies.

Shifting your mindset is the first step to changing your money patterns. The next step is upgrading small things in your life that help you hold what I like to call an *aura of abundance*. This doesn't necessarily mean having fancy cars and the most expensive clothing brands. It's about upgrading things in your life that are old, broken or that no longer hold the energy of abundance that you want to cultivate.

One day I was filling up my car, and I realised I had a pattern of only paying forty dollars' worth of fuel every time. I had a routine of fuelling my car up to three-quarters with no real reasoning or conscious thought behind it other than it supported the story of

'I still don't have enough.' Sometimes that might be the case, but on this particular day I asked myself why I was always only ever fuelling my car up three-quarters of a tank. I had more than enough money each time to pay to fill it to the brim. It was a sneaky lack habit that wasn't matching up with my new abundant reality.

This got me thinking about all the ways in our lives that we are selling ourselves short and staying stuck in lack patterns and outdated money beliefs simply out of habit. The small incremental upgrades make the biggest changes overtime, just like compound interest. When we are so used to living a certain way, we have to remind ourselves we are no longer living in struggle. It is okay to enjoy our abundance without feeling guilty about looking after ourselves and wanting to enjoy our experiences. I also noticed all the ways I was choosing the cheapest option and therefore keeping myself in an *I don't have enough* loop just to save myself a few dollars, even when it didn't make me feel good. In some cases, this is completely okay and necessary and I'm not suggesting you start throwing cash around everywhere! This is about recognising when are you living in an old outdated money pattern out of habit, rather than consciously showing up for a new one that's supporting and solidifying the direction you want to go.

Another experience I had around this was when I realised that I had been going to the same beautician since I was at uni, as she was the cheapest in my local area. This place served me well when I was a broke uni student, but I was no longer that person. I knew I needed to upgrade because every time I went there, I was no longer enjoying it. It was the type of beauty salon that was rushed, quick and gossipy, not an environment I wanted to be hanging out in anymore. For a long time, I told myself I couldn't go elsewhere because I was saving money. However, I looked up a day spa that aligned more with my values and decided it was time for a change. Who knew I could feel like a queen just from spending an extra ten dollars and choosing an experience that felt more nourishing and abundant rather than a rushing in-and-out energy that only fuelled a scarcity loop from years ago?

Think of ways you can create an aura of abundance by small upgrades at a time rather than trying to change everything in one day and becoming overwhelmed. You don't need to spend thousands of dollars to feel more abundant. Your aura of abundance isn't just about money, it's about joy and nourishment too. Stretch yourself with small comfort upgrades like your underwear, your tea towels or maybe your bed sheets. Small everyday things that will make you feel more abundant when you use them. Instead of buying ten cheap on sale items that you will probably never wear, how about buying one really beautiful item of clothing that you love and feel joyful and abundant whenever you wear it? Remember, the intention isn't about needing lots of expensive things, the key is buying more of what makes you *feel* abundant. From there, you can upgrade to things like no longer buying the red-eye flights to save yourself fifty dollars when you know that you regret it every single time. Instead of finding the cheapest hotel deal, maybe spend two nights in a less expensive place and then spend one night in a nicer place that stretches your money comfort zone just a little. You could swap shopping at the same clothing store that is your go-to for cheap deals and discounts. Try out something new that will shake your energy up. Train your brain to get comfortable with money to attract more in.

Here's where I want to plant a seed that might change the way you intentionally invest and spend money forever. Think about every time you are investing in yourself or buying something you really love. Is it solidifying your current money reality where you want to stay, or energetically preparing you for the next level? I believe we are always in practice runs and given opportunities to flex and stretch our aura of abundance. Whenever I am feeling stretched wanting to invest into the next level of my business or dreams, I ask myself this. 'Okay Trace, if you are freaking out about spending $300 right now on something you really want and love, how will you ever feel worthy and capable of spending $3000 on something you really want and love? If you can't stretch yourself to spend another $50 dollars on a flight to avoid the red-eye option, how will you ever feel okay buying business class flights?'

As I am writing this, I am thinking about all the ways I invested in myself to get to a point where investing in my dream editor didn't scare or stretch me. It was an investment for sure, but I had zero fear or resistance to it, and I would have paid double in a heartbeat. Why? Because for 5 years I have been continuously flexing my money muscles and showing up to chip away at stretching myself, all in perfect preparation for when this book deal needed to go down. Is it that you can't afford it, or that you don't feel worthy of receiving it?

◆ Rock Your Light Reflection

LIST FIVE THINGS YOU COULD UPGRADE NOW TO SHIFT YOUR OLD
MONEY MINDSET PATTERNS.

TAKE THE OPPORTUNITY NEXT TIME IT ARISES TO STRETCH YOUR
AURA OF ABUNDANCE, EVEN JUST A LITTLE SO YOU STILL STAY
GROUNDED, KNOWING EACH STRETCH IS HELPING YOU GET
STRONGER TO PREPARE FOR THE ABUNDANCE THAT'S COMING.

You are worthy of receiving.

FULL TANK.

FULL BANK.

LESSON 31

THE MONEY SHOWS UP WHEN YOU DO

It is really easy to be in the high vibes and living your most abundant life on payday or when you've just scored a large amount of cash. But the real embodiment work for abundance begins on the days when it's really inconvenient to believe in it. The days when you convince yourself that going for your dreams is too hard. That maybe the Universe doesn't want you to be successful or you're not made for this following your heart gig.

When I first started my coaching business, I was investing a lot more financially into my business and my mission than I was receiving back. When I was creating my first online coaching program, I wanted to create a video to help with the promotion. I had a clear vision and downloaded the video script within ten minutes. I knew who I wanted in it, where it would be, and exactly what it would look like. I had the vision, but not the financial input to go with it. Nevertheless, I wasn't going to cut corners. I wanted to stay true to the abundant vision I had for it. I asked the Universe for guidance, which followed with an overwhelming feeling that the money was on its way. I knew I had to bring all the pieces of the puzzle together first and then it would show up. So, I got to work contacting friends I wanted in the video, my photographer and meeting with the videographer I wanted to work with. Even though I still didn't have the money, I started coordinating things and moving energy as if I did.

A week later, Luke received a random work bonus that matched the exact dollar amount I needed for the videographer. Luke wasn't one to have conversations with about the Universe having your back at that time, but he walked in from work and said, 'Hey, here's the money for your video. I know this bonus isn't for me, it's for you.'

When you are clear on the direction you are heading and acting on, support will show up in ways that you least expect. The Universe will bring you the resources you need when you let it. Think about it as one big ocean of abundance, it just breaks into separate streams to get to you. In these moments, receive the support fully and channel it into generating more lightwork for the world. Do this, and the Universe will keep it coming, and the streams will turn into rivers.

One of the biggest ways you are keeping the Universe from being able to pour an abundance of resources into your vision and support your next steps is by continually telling yourself 'I'm not ready yet'. When you tell yourself that story, you are most probably staying in a cycle of inaction and procrastination. The Universe has no choice but to follow suit and procrastinate on bringing you the resources you require because you're energetically saying, 'I'm not ready for the Universe to support my dreams yet.'

As a lightworker who is committed to living a heart-driven life, you need to master the art of trusting your intuition when it doesn't make logical, linear sense. To keep moving forward, you must learn to create beyond your current reality and reach for new beliefs and possibilities. Your visions and dreams aren't just yours; they are the Universe's dreams for you. So, what if you believe, and deeply know, the Universe can only show up for you, when you show up for the Universe?

Stop judging where the support is coming from! It might come through family members, friends, the government, your current workplace, or a refund you weren't expecting. Remember that it's all coming from the same source, just in different packaging.

Rock Your Light Affirmation

THE UNIVERSE SUPPORTS MY DREAMS.

INTUITION OPENS THE GATES TO
ABUNDANCE,
ACTION ON THAT INTUITION
OPENS IT WIDER.

LESSON 32

ABUNDANCE FLOWS FASTER THROUGH A CLEAR CHANNEL

You know that feeling when you are trying to find something in your house, and you want to give up because it becomes such a mission. You are stepping over boxes, climbing over piles of stuff, then you trip over some shoes that are lying around. Suddenly, you're on an obstacle course just to find a piece of paper you wrote something important on. Money feels the same way when you don't have clear instructions and channels for it to flow into your life, your business and your bank account. You've got to make it really easy for money to flow to you because abundance doesn't like to be confused or restricted, it wants space to flow with ease.

Let's take a moment here to think about all the creative ways that money hangs out in your life right now, and more specifically the containers it is hanging out in. Is your wallet old, falling apart with broken zips and overflowing with old cards and receipts you don't need or use? Do you love your wallet when you look at it? Think of your wallet as one of your most important money containers. Is there even space in there for money to stay, or will it fall straight out again?

Now think about your bank accounts. Do you have clear intentions with each of them? Do you know what they are all for? Are there still accounts with ex-partners that need closing, or accounts that you don't intend on putting money into? Think about the savings accounts you are constantly looking at each time you log on to check your accounts and you aren't even using them. So, your money story of 'I don't have any savings' keeps repeating in your reality because you aren't really intentionally using your savings account. Having multiple empty, or unnecessary bank accounts is a sneaky money leak that needs to be plugged up so that money knows you will hold it safely.

Abundance doesn't like confusion; it wants clear direction and a spacious container.

One of the first things I encourage my coaching clients to do is to take a little look at all the pathways that abundance travels through their business. I ask them if it is a clear and direct channel, without physical or energetic trip hazards along the way.

Do you have the right systems and structures set up for clients to pay you easily, or are there back-and-forth emails before this happens? Are your payment details crystal clear? Are you always avoiding money conversations and letting someone else do it for you: a receptionist, a personal assistant, your parents? If you have a healing space or your office at home, even if you take clients online, is there a clear pathway from the front door to the space you work so that clients have a clear path to find you? Are you holding onto things from old businesses that failed, rather than clearing the slate and being all in—mentally, physically and energetically—on your current business? Or is there a part of you holding onto the past just in case?

I was explaining this concept to a close friend who is an artist and has a home studio stacked with her gorgeous artwork and paintings. Although she was selling her art online, I explained the energetics to her. She still needed to clean out the clutter in her studio and have some paintings she wanted to sell within view and easily accessible. This way, she was stating to the Universe 'these are ready to be seen and sent to their new homes', rather than collecting dust in a pile in the corner of the room. She later told me she cleaned up her studio, and soon after sold three of her biggest paintings.

Rock Your Light Reflection

LOOK AT ALL THE WAYS MONEY IS TRYING TO FLOW TO YOU AND STAY WITH YOU. ARE ANY TRIP HAZARDS KEEPING MONEY FROM HAVING A CLEAR CHANNEL TO FLOW?

Clean up your trip hazards to make it easy for money to run to you.

ABUNDANCE
LOVES CLARITY.

LESSON 33

FORGIVENESS OPENS THE FLOODGATES

One of the biggest blocks we have around money flowing into our lives is the underlying judgements and fear that we don't trust ourselves with money. Maybe you've had negative experiences with money in the past, so you gave up on your relationship with money and just accepted that it was bad. Many lightworkers today had a lot of power in a past life, and they abused it. We didn't understand what it meant to have abundance, and we didn't know what to do with it when we had it.

This lifetime is about trusting ourselves with power and abundance again, knowing that we will always use money with the highest intentions to create more good in the world. If we are holding judgement, blame, anger or frustration in our hearts from the past about money, we are creating an energetic resistance that is stopping more money from flowing in.

It's all well and good to be repeating your 'money flows easily to me' affirmations. But the energy in your body that reacts to money every time you think about it is the one that's running the show here. As you read in lesson 32, money wants a clear channel and a clear container to flow through and into. Your negative feelings towards money are a big tripping hazard keeping the door of abundance closed until further notice.

One exercise that I highly encourage you do if you have a lot of icky feelings towards money, is some money forgiveness. Straight away your ego might say, 'Money has only ever created bad things in my life, as if I'm going to forgive it.' I encourage you to show up anyway to this exercise and see what unravels for you. As you will soon see, this isn't about forgiving *money*, it's about forgiving *yourself*.

Rock Your Light Reflection

GRAB A JOURNAL, A PEN AND GET READY TO SET A TIMER FOR
TEN MINUTES.

TAKE THIS TIME TO WRITE OUT ANY MONEY EXPERIENCES THAT
YOU WANT TO LET GO OF. FREE WRITE THEM DOWN, THIS MEANS
NO READING BACK OVER OR EDITING,
JUST WRITE FROM THE HEART.

YOUR MONEY FORGIVENESS WRITING MIGHT GO
SOMETHING LIKE THIS. . .

I FORGIVE MYSELF FOR LYING ABOUT MY DEBT AND PRETENDING
IT'S NOT THERE.

I FORGIVE MYSELF FOR STEALING MONEY WHEN I WAS YOUNGER.

I FORGIVE MYSELF FOR DEMANDING MORE MONEY WITHOUT BEING
GRATEFUL FOR WHAT I HAD.

I FORGIVE MYSELF FOR BLAMING MONEY FOR MY RELATIONSHIP PROBLEMS.

I FORGIVE MYSELF FOR UNDERCHARGING MY WORTH AND LETTING PEOPLE RIP ME OFF.

I FORGIVE MYSELF FOR PRETENDING THAT I DON'T CARE ABOUT MONEY.

I FORGIVE MYSELF FOR SPENDING MY INHERITANCE ON THINGS THAT WEREN'T GOOD FOR ME.

I FORGIVE MYSELF FOR NOT HAVING ANY SAVINGS AND BEING KNOWN AS THE BROKE FRIEND.

I FORGIVE MYSELF FOR USING MONEY AS AN EXCUSE FOR THE REASON I WON'T CHASE MY DREAMS.

I FORGIVE MYSELF FOR JUDGING OTHER PEOPLE WHO HAVE MONEY.

I FORGIVE MYSELF FOR THAT POOR BUSINESS DEAL I MADE THAT COST ME A LOT OF MONEY.

I FORGIVE MYSELF FOR THINKING MONEY IS EVIL AND JUDGING EVERYONE WHO HAS MORE THAN I DO.

I FORGIVE MYSELF FOR WAITING FOR SOMEBODY ELSE TO COME AND FIX MY MONEY PROBLEMS FOR ME.

I FORGIVE MYSELF FOR BLAMING MY PARENTS, INSTEAD OF BEING RESPONSIBLE FOR MY OWN MONEY.

I FORGIVE MYSELF FOR CHOOSING AN ACCOUNTANT WHO MADE ERRORS AND COST ME MONEY.

I FORGIVE MYSELF FOR TELLING MYSELF I'M DUMB RATHER THAN LEARNING ABOUT MONEY.

I FORGIVE MYSELF FOR MISUSING POWER AND WEALTH IN A PAST LIFE, EVEN IF I CAN'T REMEMBER IT.

✦

WRITE DOWN EVERY SINGLE ICKY MONEY FEELING, THOUGHT OR EXPERIENCE, BEING AS SPECIFIC AS YOU CAN. I HOPE YOU FEEL A LITTLE LIGHTER AFTER DOING THIS EXERCISE. WHEN YOU FORGIVE YOURSELF AND TAKE THE ENERGETIC CHARGE OFF THESE MONEY EXPERIENCES, YOU DROP YOUR RESISTANCE TO MONEY AND ALLOW IT TO FEEL MORE JOYFUL AND EXCITING AGAIN.

**I forgive myself and allow
money to flow freely to me.**

IT'S SAFE
FOR ME TO RECEIVE
ABUNDANTLY
FOR MY GREAT WORK.

LESSON 34

ABUNDANTLY GIVE AND YOU WILL BE ABUNDANTLY GIVEN TO

We are in a pivotal time where all of us are feeling the pressure and the inner call to step up into our potential and higher purpose to help others do the same. We want to help and we want to create change. And we want to do our best and be of service to the world, but sometimes we can let our ego run wild with the story we are never-doing-enough.

Your lightwork is your lifework. It's just who you are. You don't need to track hours and clock in and out of your lightwork. Bring your radiant energy everywhere you go. Let it naturally pour through you. Stop worrying about how it looks or where your light is currently being required and focus on turning it up. Now, this isn't talk about burning out and having no boundaries. This is a conversation about not holding back when there are opportunities being presented to share your *light* and offer support to someone in need.

When I first started my business, I would speak to anyone who would listen. I would write countless social media posts sharing pieces of information and tools that were helping me on my inner journey, hoping they would inspire and help someone else on theirs. I was abundantly sharing without needing anything back, just for the joy of sharing my truth. I got out of the way and let the Universe work through me because I had this overwhelming feeling that I had to keep helping however I could.

After years of grounding into my gifts, collecting evidence that my message was resonating with people and building my confidence as a speaker and teacher, it then came to a point where I was ready to receive in exchange for my serving. I knew I'd done the groundwork, and I was open and ready to receive for my great work with zero guilt.

It's easy for our ego to block our flow by always thinking 'what's in it for me' or, complaining that we aren't receiving enough, without checking in with how much value we are giving in return.

Think of how you have helped someone out without expecting anything in return, and then the support has been returned in other ways. Through someone buying you coffee or offering you a free yoga session, or you jump online, and someone has shared your work with their community when you never asked or had expectations.

Pour your *full* heart in and let the Universe *fill* in the gaps.

✦ Rock Your Light Reflection

HOW CAN YOU REACH MORE PEOPLE WITH YOUR GIVING? HOW CAN YOU HELP A FRIEND IN NEED? HOW CAN YOU SHARE SOMEONE ELSE'S WORK WHO IS REALLY INSPIRING YOU ON OUR JOURNEY? WHERE CAN YOU DONATE TO A CHARITY THAT IS DOING GREAT WORK IN THE WORLD? WHERE CAN YOU OFFER FREE ONLINE YOGA VIDEOS OR GUIDED MEDITATIONS BEFORE NEEDING TO TURN THEM INTO AN INCOME STREAM?

SIDE NOTE: THE MONEY AND ABUNDANCE WILL ALL COME WHEN IT'S MEANT TO.

Your lightwork is your lifework.

IF YOU ONLY SHARE <u>HALF</u> OF YOUR *gifts*,
THE UNIVERSE WILL ONLY SHARE HALF OF *its gifts* WITH YOU.

LESSON 35

THE HELPERS ARE ALWAYS HELPED

The first time I read the words THE HELPERS ARE ALWAYS HELPED on the back of an angel card, I cried. It was one of those moments where the right words find you at exactly the right time you are open and ready to receive them.

It was a moment that I was so close to giving up because I felt like I had been pouring so much into my dreams, but not yet fully reaping the rewards. I knew they were on their way, but my belief in myself to keep charging forward was feeling thin that day. I had such big dreams that felt so clear in my heart, but I still felt so far away from them.

There have been so many times along my path where I didn't know how I would make it work. I've lost count of the amount of times I've drained my bank accounts to follow my intuition and invest in the next step in my journey that the Universe was guiding me towards. Whether it was trainings, courses, coaches, books, I was showing up to every single piece of guidance the Universe was gifting me.

But that day, I was scared. What if the money doesn't show up? What if my dreams never come true? Am I the right person for this job? What if I'm just not meant to be successful in the way my heart is telling me I can be? What if I never get there? *Universe, I'm scared. I can't do this on my own anymore.*

The helpers are always helped, Trace. You just have to ask.

In that moment, I'd forgotten that I wasn't alone in my mission. I wasn't meant to do this all by myself. In fact, I couldn't. It was time to let the Universe support me in ways I could never have supported myself.

It takes courage to keep showing up when there are people around you that are telling you you're crazy. It takes courage to keep going when you are feeling like nothing is moving forward and no one is getting it. It takes courage to choose belief over fear time and time again. It takes courage to show up fully for your dreams in a world that constantly tells you it's not safe or responsible to do so. It takes courage to invest in your dreams and lean so deeply into the abundance of your vision before it shows up in your reality. It takes courage to commit to living your lightwork.

But courage, my friend, is exactly what being a lightworker is all about.

Courage is in your blood. It's what you signed up for in this lifetime. You didn't come here to let your gifts go to waste and wait until you had all of your shit together. You didn't come here to procrastinate and play small. And you definitely didn't come here to mess around and hide your true self from the world.

You came here to create from your heart, to be abundantly sup-ported in your unique gifts, and to unapologetically *rock your light* with the world. Do this with the full knowing that when you allow yourself to do so, you give others permission to rock their light and live their truth too.

No one is stopping you but you. Lean on the lessons in this book to keep you moving forward on your mission and support you in living with greater purpose, power and prosperity in exactly the way you intended to this lifetime.

Make the commitment to yourself that you will never stop growing, creating, serving and showing up to the inner guidance of your heart with the full knowing that the helpers are always helped.

The Universe is committed to your lightwork.
Please.
Just.
Keep.
Going.

THE HELPERS ARE
ALWAYS HELPED.

PROSPERITY POEM

Give the Universe a chance to support you; get out of the way,
and go all in on your dreams.
Spend less time crunching numbers,
and more time cracking hearts open.
Keep working on your radiance, and not just your resume.
Trust in your lightwork, because when you are lit up,
you will light up everyone around you.

There's a secret to abundance: you have so much to give,
just as you are, so move now with what you've got.
More will come, know that the Universe is rooting for you.
It is highly invested in your success,
even when you think it's not, it is.
The money will show up when you do, let your heart lead,
and leave your ego at the door.

Be generous with your light, don't keep it all to yourself,
because when you let it pour out of you, you open for more to pour
in,
Not just to your heart, but to your bank account too,
Open your hands and heart wider, receive all that is here for you.
Your dreams are waiting for you to say yes, it's never just a yes for you,
it's a yes for the whole world.

ACKNOWLEDGEMENTS

For a long time, I felt like I had to do this work alone. It wasn't until I let other people help that I could truly spread my wings and soar. This book is because of the many incredible people who have helped me along the way.

I want to thank one particular person who saw my light even before I did. My mentor of seven years now, who I choose to respect his privacy and not mention his name here. You know who you are.

I thank Anita Tropiano for taking me under her wing and giving me the nudge to teach and share my work before I felt ready to. Thank you from the bottom of my heart for believing in me.

Julie Parker, because of your courage to follow your heart's vision to create the Beautiful You Coaching Academy, I remembered who I was and stepped boldly into my purpose as a lightworker. I thank you.

Rachel MacDonald, thank you for inspiring me to start blogging many years ago. Hitting publish on that first blog post was the draft copy that allowed me to hit publish on this first book.

Tara Bliss, thank you for teaching me about leadership, for believing in my heart and constantly reflecting my potential back to me.

I want to send gratitude to my spiritual running buddies who have believed in me and cheered me on from the very beginning, Kurt Tropiano, Sammie Fleming, Hellè Weston, Zsuzsa Octaviano, Victoria Bauman, Heidi Anderson, Amanda Hill and Ellie Swift who have poured their genuine love, support and energy my way.

I want to thank my dream editor Natasha Gilmour, who never once tried to change my voice and only encouraged me to be more of myself through this writing process. Thank you for helping me stay true to the vision of this book and for gently, yet powerfully, offering words of wisdom to soften my self-doubt through the writing of my first book.

Thank you to Elle for putting up with my creative chaos whilst bringing the cover and look of this book to life, especially the time I messaged you at midnight with, 'Hey, can we add poems to the book cover?' I love making magic with you!

I thank my parents, David and Robin, who love and accept that I am the crazy hippie one in the family and who cheer me on in my dreams no matter what.

A huge shout out to my incredible fiancé and partner in shine, Luke, who has never ever tried to clip my wings and continues to encourage me to go bigger with my dreams.

Finally, I thank you, my reader. You inspire me to keep showing up so fiercely for my lightwork. I will never stop rocking my light in the hope that it will give you full permission to unapologetically rock yours too.

LIGHTWORKER
RESOURCES

Head to www.rockyourlight.com.au to download a bunch of incredible tools to help you on your lightworking journey.

You can listen to Tracey's Live Your Lightwork Podcast on iTunes and Spotify.

To step up and go big with your lightwork, check out Tracey's four-month transformational online program, Lightworkers Academy:
www.lightworkersacademy.com.au

FIND TRACEY AT
www.traceyspencer.com.au

INSTAGRAM
@tracey___spencer
#rockyourlightbook

ABOUT THE AUTHOR

Tracey Spencer is an award-winning creative business coach, author, speaker and kundalini yoga teacher who is on a mission to help women eliminate self-doubt and go big with their lightwork.

Through her 1:1 mentoring, Lightworkers Academy and Business Sistermind online programs, podcast, live workshops and her straight talking Instagram stories, Tracey offers real courage for you to take action on your dreams.

Winner of the 2014-2016 *Beautiful You* Emerging Coach of The Year Award, Tracey reminds you how much of a privilege it is to be you, and shows you how to rock your light, lead from the heart and make an impact on the lives around you.

Lightning Source UK Ltd.
Milton Keynes UK
UKHW011459250722
406336UK00002B/527